Dr. Brent Price has charted an effective soulwinning road map for pointing people to the way of salvation in Jesus Christ. His passion and purity of motive are unquestioned, and his desire to facilitate equipping God's people is a proven pastoral track of his ministry.

—Dr. Jack Hayford
Founder, Church on the Way
President
International Church of the Foursquare Gospel

I personally congratulate Dr. Brent Price for this incisive and very timely source for personal evangelism. Jesus and Socrates agreed: "Ask questions and listen for the answers." And Jesus answered, "Be ready to give an answer to every man that asketh thee for the hope within you." It's ingenious, it's scriptural, and it works for anyone!

—Pat Boone
Internationally Known Entertainer

Dr. Brent Price has created a biblical soulwinning plan named the *Witnessing Winzone* that is marvelous in its simplicity and effectiveness. Believers can now quickly learn how to start winning souls in personal evangelism. It is a powerful tool to lead the unsaved to decisions for Jesus Christ in the twenty-first century.

—Bishop Charles E. Blake
Pastor
West Angeles Church of God in Christ

I have just finished reading Brent Price's new book, *Witnessing Winzone*. It is absolutely wonderful…a breath of fresh air…exciting, biblical, stimulating, and right on!

—Dr. John R. Bisagno
Former Pastor
First Baptist Church Houston

Brent Price has created a primer that provides a practical guide for introducing people to the transforming power of the gospel. The content of this *Soulwinner's Handbook* is biblically grounded, and the content of communication is open, dialogical, and exploratory in finding the *Witnessing Winzone*. This book is must-reading for those who want to share the message of God's salvation in Jesus Christ in an effective, genuine, and Spirit-led manner.

—Dr. Murray W. Dempster
President
Vanguard University
Costa Mesa, California

Brent Price has done us all a favor by taking what is a challenge for most of us and simplifying it. He teaches us how to turn a conversation into a conversion possibility. He makes every conversation a witnessing opportunity and helps us to bring people to a place where they will accept Jesus as their Savior.

—Pastor Gary Cooper
Breakthrough Foursquare Church
Culver City, California

Dr. Brent Price has created the simplest and most effective way imaginable to learn how to win souls. It doesn't matter if you are in the lunchroom or the boardroom, this is your answer to winning souls. Through the *Witnessing Winzone* and his soulwinning seminars, Brent Price is the expert, the "go-to guy" to learn how to win souls.

—Pastor Steve Weller
Venice Foursquare Church
Venice, California
National Founder, Addicts for Christ

Dr. Brent Price practices what he preaches! He not only knows how to witness in a unique way, he knows how to teach others to witness and win souls in a powerful and usable way. He is a witnessing man of God and I've even watched him win souls on a golf course! His book and seminar will teach you how to be a mighty witness for the kingdom of God.

—Pastor Fred Barber
Living Branch Foursquare Church
Culver City, California

Let's cut to the chase. The church of Jesus Christ—at least in America—is not cutting it. We need help. Lots of help. Most churches are not seeing authentic evangelistic growth. Many believers are not effectively sharing the basics of their faith in compelling and magnetic ways. We acknowledge our need for help. Brent Price functions as a "conscience," gently, but persistently, reminding us, "You have something precious to share. So here's how to do it."

—Dr. Jim Garlow
Senior Pastor, Skyline Wesleyan Church
La Mesa, California

Dr. Brent Price, through the *Witnessing Winzone*, leads us step by step with a treasure trove of scripture on the enormous importance of how to lead the lost to salvation. A must read for everyone, including all Christians, pastors, and churches.

—Al Kasha
Two-time Academy Award winning composer, author, and
ordained minister

# WITNESSING WINZONE

## BRENT PRICE, D.MIN.

CREATION
HOUSE
A STRANG COMPANY

WITNESSING WINZONE by Brent Price
Published by Creation House
A Strang Company
600 Rinehart Road
Lake Mary, Florida 32746
www.creationhouse.com

Unless otherwise noted, Scripture quotations are from the New
King James Version of the Bible. Copyright © 1979, 1980, 1982
by Thomas Nelson, Inc., publishers. Used by permission.

Scripture quotations marked KJV are from the King James Version
of the Bible.

Cover design by Terry Clifton

Library of Congress Control Number: 2005924888
International Standard Book Number: 1-59185-812-7

05 06 07 08 09 — 987654321
Printed in the United States of America

# Dedication

To my wonderful wife, Beverly. I love you and know that God called us as husband and wife. Thank you for sharing a life journey with me and giving me your love, fun, fellowship, and a beautiful daughter. Thank you for your patience as I labored over this book and for the many times we "brainstormed" about soulwinning ideas.

To my daughter, Brittney. Your mother and I love and adore you. I am very proud of you and I know the Lord has great things in store for you. At a young age you came to Christ and learned about life commitments, and I am thrilled to be your father.

To my father, Eldon Andrew Price. Even though you have gone to be with the Lord you are always in my thoughts. I miss you and look forward to days in heaven when I can be with you again.

To my mother, Thelma Rose Price. All of my life I have known that you believed in me. Thank you for a mother's special love that I have cherished every day of my life.

To my two sisters, Sandy Perkins and Cheryl Pany. I love you both! Separated only by distance, I look forward to our times together. In your different ways you are both remarkable women and I am proud to be your brother.

# Acknowledgments

To Dr. Jack Hayford, founder of Church on the Way, Van Nuys, California, and President of Foursquare International, whose counsel, direction, and encouragement helped me to write *Witnessing Winzone*. He is my former pastor, a father in the faith to many, and I believe, the preeminent pastoral theologian of our era.

To John R. Webb Jr., a beloved brother and friend who was a Christian role model for me when I was first saved. John was the first person to help me understand I could win someone to Jesus Christ. Thank you for your years of friendship, counsel, and editing help on this book.

To Rev. Buford E. Cain, former pastor of Easthaven Baptist Church, Houston, Texas. It was your advice one Monday morning that the Lord used to launch me toward a life in ministry and ultimately to author the *Witnessing Winzone*.

To Dr. David Conrad whom the Lord used to first get me excited about developing a soulwinning plan.

To Pastor Gary and Carolyn Cooper for your time and help in the editing process. Thank you for your counsel, patience, and help.

To Dr. Daniel Goldberg, my dissertation mentor at California Pacific School of Theology, Glendale, California. Thank you for your encouragement and direction.

To the people of First United Methodist Church of Lockhart, Texas, a glorious church filled with precious memories. You, along with my mother and father, built a foundation of the things of God in me.

Last, but certainly not least, to the people of Beverly Hills Foursquare Church, Beverly Hills, California. I have the privilege of being your pastor and I love you with all my heart.

# Contents

# Foreword

WHEN I MET BRENT PRICE, he was Pastor of the Singles Department in a huge Baptist Church—a guy with a heart for people and a passion for seeing souls brought to Jesus. Later, when he opened to the dimensions of the Holy Spirit's gifts he moved into his own pastorate—losing nothing of his love for people and desire to find ways to reach them, but bringing to a new arena his creative pursuit of winning souls.

Historically, there is no part of Christ's body more systematic or strategic about evangelism than Southern Baptists. Presently, there is no part of the church where that same zeal might find a home than in your heart or mine—whether we are Charismatic or Presbyterian, Pentecostal or Methodist, Episcopal or Evangelical Free, or any other sector of God's great family, from Catholic to Orthodox, from Christian Church to Brethren...and the list goes on.

This book is a pointer and a practical guide. This book is a summons and a summary—a handbook that holds helps that every believer needs and many do not have. This book reminds us that we are all—and always—to "be ready to give everyone who asks us, an answer—a reason for the hope we have in Christ."

Witnessing, soulwinning, evangelizing—whatever term we use—is an assignment given to every one of us. First Peter 3:15, paraphrased above, is the practical application of the Great

Commission at a personal level. We are to reach "all the world" on the basis of "one at a time"—where we live, work, and meet people. To "be ready" requires (a.) a *familiarity* with the basics (which should never be presumed), and (b.) a *functionality* with a plan (which the Holy Spirit will help you adapt to each situation in which He opens a doorway to "give an answer . . . a reason . . . a hope" to people living in a hopeless world.

Today, Brent Price continues touching people for Jesus—one at a time. He is the pastor of the Foursquare Church in Beverly Hills, California, and he conveys a gracious and grace-attended ministry where souls are not only saved, but also where the life of Jesus is ministered at every dimension by the power of the Holy Spirit.

My own convictions are that every believer needs help in formulating an approach for conversing with people about Jesus. I am hesitant to promote the idea of *imposing* a witness on anyone, but equally unwilling to presume *supposing* I can "be ready," as the Bible says, unless I have (a.) *a grasp of the biblical elements* of soul-saving truth, and (b.) *a grip on a winsome approach* that will help me target the message home to human hearts.

Brent Price has not only provided us with these key elements to equip and resource us. He has also proven their effectiveness, in his own lifestyle of faithfully leading many to Christ as well as in the life of a host of other believers he has helped to a witness readiness and a soulwinning effectiveness.

—DR. JACK W. HAYFORD
CHANCELLOR, THE KING'S COLLEGE AND SEMINARY
PRESIDENT
INTERNATIONAL CHURCH OF THE FOURSQUARE GOSPEL
FOUNDER, THE CHURCH ON THE WAY
VAN NUYS, CALIFORNIA

# 1

# The Soulwinning Solution

## LEARNING HOW TO WIN
## SOULS THROUGH PERSONAL EVANGELISM

THE VISION OF THE *Witnessing Winzone* is to successfully equip multitudes of mature teen and adult believers to win souls in personal evangelism. It incorporates a soulwinning plan that utilizes a unique biblical strategy to lead unbelievers to salvation in Jesus Christ. The plan was designed for believers to easily implement during typical witnessing or any kind of a faith-sharing exchange. This unique plan and strategy will equip any believer to win souls as they face a variety of twenty-first century challenges. Believers will quickly discover that this biblical soulwinning plan and strategy is brief, uncomplicated, and very successful.

*Witnessing Winzone* represents the soulwinning plan. Witnessing is presenting the claims of Jesus Christ to unbelievers. *Winzone* is a word I developed because of the function of the words *win* and *zone*. *Win* refers to winning a soul, and *zone* relates to the strategic framework of the soulwinning plan. Together, they represent the witnessing dynamic of winning a soul to Jesus Christ. The component that starts the *Winzone* is a simple transition from a typical witnessing exchange into an intentional soulwinning sequence in the plan. This transition is vitally important because typical witness exchanges rarely have salvation conclusions. The exciting result of this unique transitional process is the creation of a teachable moment in an unbeliever. A teachable moment is an amazing moment when suddenly, an unbeliever becomes very receptive to hearing the salvation gospel of Jesus Christ. The soulwinning plan and strategy equips and prepares believers to create teachable moments, present the salvation gospel, and effortlessly lead unbelievers to salvation.

Regardless of denomination or church affiliation, any believer can become thoroughly equipped to win souls with this flexible soulwinning plan. A large portion of becoming equipped is getting solid answers to a host of personal evangelism concerns that are normally overwhelming. These are about issues that all believers face in personal evangelism—concerns that for many believers have brought personal evangelism to a complete standstill. Believers will discover solid common sense answers and insights, refined from over twenty years of my own successful soulwinning experiences.

Another of the most exciting results of this soulwinning plan is that it eliminates fear, confusion, and intimidation in the witnessing and soulwinning process. Newly equipped believers experience breakthroughs from fear and doubt, into a confident sense of personal assurance in personal evangelism. Also, believers just like you immediately develop a positive attitude about engaging in witnessing conversations. Actually learning how to win souls—not just thinking and talking about it—is now a very realistic and achievable goal for believers in Jesus Christ.

Significant segments of the *Witnessing Winzone* will also deal with the meaning of different evangelistic terms and phrases. Throughout the body of Christ, such terms as personal evangelism, witnessing, soulwinning, sharing your faith, sharing personal testimony, sowing, reaping, and discipleship can all have slightly different meanings to believers from different church backgrounds. Believers will gain a bold assurance as these terms are clearly defined for personal application. These definitions have no denominational or theological bias but only a common application to equip believers to win souls in personal evangelism.

Ultimately, the *Witnessing Winzone* soulwinning plan solves all the problems that are at the core of why most believers do not witness or win souls. Believers face many challenges and many more are addressed in a later chapter, but the main obstacle for believers comes from the simple exortation to "witness or share your faith." This sounds simple enough, but the reality is that every evangelical believer knows that the expected result from witnessing or sharing their faith is for them to win souls.

When encouraged to witness or share their faith, believers hear the subtle implication that they must create their own soulwinning plan or method for personal evangelism. After that, to support their newly self-invented plan, they also hear that they will have to become a Bible expert in order to answer any and all questions from an unbeliever. They further hear that without a special "evangelism gift" they are going to have to have the ability to "outtalk" unbelievers into receiving Jesus Christ as Savior. What they hear is that they are pretty much on their own in personal evangelism. These challenges by themselves are what bring most believers to a complete standstill in personal evangelism. The answers to these core problems and many more are all solved when believers become equipped with this completely prepared soulwinning plan. It is a plan that reflects a solid biblical strategy that is highly successful and easy to learn.

## My Soulwinning Learning Curve

The *Witnessing Winzone* plan is an outgrowth of an earlier soulwinning plan that I first began developing for my personal use for an evangelistic outreach at the 1984 Olympics in Los Angeles, California. As a Minister to Singles at First Baptist Van Nuys in Van Nuys, California, I served under the senior pastor, Dr. Jess Moody, who has a passion for winning souls, for discipleship, and to see believers equipped to win souls. One Sunday in May of 1984, I was notified that a group called *Lay Witness for Christ* was coming to the church. This evangelistic group had a ministry to athletes at the collegiate and professional level. They were going to minister at the 1984 Olympics games in Los Angeles and were going to make our church their headquarters for the event. When the invitation came to attend an introductory training meeting to learn how to witness at the Olympic Village, I felt this would be a tremendous experience for our Singles Group. I promoted the event to them and several responded. However, I had no idea God was preparing a divine encounter that would change my life forever.

During this training session, many of us heard for the first time a planned gospel presentation for winning souls. Dr. David Conrad, the associate pastor at United Community Church in Glendale, California, taught the course. Instead of talking about general witnessing ideas and concepts, he began to teach a method of winning souls he had developed for his own use as he counseled church visitors in his office. As I listened, I realized that for the first time in my life I was hearing a lengthy, but step-by-step gospel presentation, that had a beginning, middle, and planned conclusion. Dr. Conrad's witnessing model was, according to him, clear to the unbeliever and therefore, one that he felt comfortable using.

I had worked in the sales field for several years and knew a presentation with a close when I heard one. While I understood that this was not a sales presentation, it was a presentation of the gospel for salvation leading toward a point of planned closure and resulting in an opportunity for an unbeliever to receive salvation. I was intrigued with Dr. Conrad's presentation, and after the meeting I approached him and asked if I could come to his office to personally discuss more about winning souls. He agreed and we had the first of several private witnessing/soulwinning brainstorming sessions. As I mentioned, these sessions were arranged just before the outreach at the Olympic Village that summer of 1984. The Lord used lay-witness for Christ, David Conrad, and those Olympics to get me serious and committed about learning how to win souls. I have never lost that commitment.

## Olympians Broke Records, I Broke Through, and So Can You!

On the Saturday scheduled for the Olympic outreach, I was excited and a bit nervous to try out some of my new ideas. I was not sure what would happen, because I had never attempted to approach a complete stranger with the purpose of witnessing to them. I just knew I wanted to test my newly acquired insights about sharing the gospel with unbelievers.

I joined the group who had volunteered to be involved in this witnessing event, and when we had all paired off, we agreed to meet back at the Southern Baptist venue in three hours. We just sort of took off in different directions and began to melt into the crowd. Talk about a crowd! There were thousands of people coming and going, trading pins and whatever else someone was willing to trade—people from all over the world. As it turned out, I was the only staff pastor from our church, and I asked the leader of the *Lay Witness for Christ* group if I could accompany him and observe what he did and said.

The plan was to hand out flyers advertising a later event that involved an Olympics' athlete, Carl Lewis. *Lay Witness For Christ* had ministered to Carl Lewis (who won four gold medals at these summer games). And Carl was going to share his testimony during a special service at our church. We were going to hand out flyers advertising that event with the idea of taking that opportunity to initiate a conversation and witness to unbelievers. This evangelistic outreach was thrilling. People were bristling with excitement at being a part of the Olympic games, hurrying from one venue to another, but unfortunately, they had no time for the flyers my partner was trying to hand out. As I followed along, trying to engage people with our invitations, no one would even take a flyer, much less stop long enough for a conversation.

After a while I sensed the Lord leading me to separate myself and go off alone. As I walked toward the Olympic Coliseum, I came to a huge open area that was like a gigantic picnic ground. Thousands of people were sitting around eating or just relaxing. In this area, they were sitting still; what they were not doing was moving! This was my chance to approach whomever I wanted, and that is what I did. I trusted the leading of the Holy Spirit and began to talk with different people. I used the Carl Lewis flyer to engage people and initiate witnessing conversations. It was a very successful afternoon.

Time passed quickly, and I returned to our meeting place at the scheduled hour. Everyone was excited about all the people they had witnessed to and invited to the special meeting. When they asked me how I did, I reported that I had led nine people to the Lord. Several looked at me like, *Are you kidding?* As it turned out, there was a lot of witnessing activity that day, but no other soul-winning results.

## GREAT EXPERIENCE—BUT IT'S OVER

The next day was Sunday and I was busy as usual at church with all its activities. I had mentally brushed aside what I experienced at the Olympics the day before—until that night. Later that evening, as I reflected later on what had happened the day before, I became convinced that the Lord was calling me to return to the Olympic Village to witness and win more souls. So I responded, going alone, and before the week was over, I had led a total of 105 people to salvation in Jesus Christ—people from all over the world. As I led people to the Lord, I would fill out the traditional follow-up cards and turn them in to the Southern Baptist venue.

That is how the Lord gave me a breakthrough in learning how to win souls during those exciting days at the Olympic Games. It was then that He first began to lead me to develop what has become a very flexible and successful soulwinning plan. After that great experience at the Summer Olympics, it took a long time to develop the next level of the soulwinning plan. Since everyone to whom I had witnessed and won to Christ at the Olympics was introduced to the subject by our invitation to come and hear gold-medal-winner Carl Lewis speak, without a Carl Lewis and an

Olympics I had a problem. The problem was what to use as a tool to engage people in conversation about the Lord in order to regain the success results I enjoyed from the Olympic outreach.

Through trial and error, using different designs over a period of time, I was able to overcome this problem. I was able to formulate a biblically strategic soulwinning plan, which I call the *Witnessing Winzone*, that has for many years been highly effective and is easy to duplicate. Any believer can learn it without having to go through the frustration and struggles that I did. Because it is a precise and simple soulwinning strategy, it quickly produces salvation results. I continue to win souls with ease using this biblical strategy.

Those early successful experiences became a personal life-changing breakthrough in learning how to win souls. The strategy formulated over the years is a strategic biblical method to win souls in any witnessing exchange. It is a strategy that provides clarity in how to bring a soulwinning "close," so to speak, in casual/typical witnessing exchanges! Over the years I have led countless numbers to Christ and trained many others to win souls, using this soulwinning plan that you are about to learn. In the same way that I experienced my breakthrough, so can you!

## GENERAL WITNESSING OR WINNING SOULS?

There is a vast difference between general witnessing conversation with a person, what I call *casual or typical witnessing*, and actually winning souls. As you learn to win souls, you will clearly experience this difference. Broader explanations follow, but the basic difference can be defined as follows:

- *Casual/typical witnessing* is when a believer shares about the things of God with which he or she is familiar. Witnessing is usually part of a relationship building process. The believer might share a personal testimony concerning something of God that has affected them. This kind of sharing almost never has a point of closure resulting in an unsaved person receiving Christ. On the contrary, general witnessing can at times go on and on, sometimes including subtle debates that become sort of a verbal tap dance about a variety of issues. It may include invitations to visit a church or Bible study, but is usually an ongoing general conversation about the things of God and Jesus Christ.

- *Winning a soul* involves bringing the witnessing process to a point of closure with an unbeliever praying to receive salvation. This is when a believer leads an unbeliever to receive Jesus Christ as Savior. Typically, this result happens in the power of the Spirit and there is a specific goal to bring casual witnessing to salvation closure. If a believer has an effective soulwinning plan, concept, or technique, winning souls is not hard. Whenever the gospel is presented sensitively and correctly, winning a soul will be the result, and an unsaved person will receive Christ.

## Foundation of love

Whenever a believer attempts to share his or her faith personally, to be a witness and win souls, they must always do so in love. A relationship with an unbeliever, whether of short or long duration, must be rooted in love. The foundation for success in witnessing is love, allowing unbelievers to perceive that what they are being told is grounded in love. They must have a sense that they are cared for and loved. The apostle Paul wrote:

> Though I speak with the tongues of men and of angels, but have not love, I have become sounding brass or a clanging cymbal. And though I have the gift of prophecy, and understand all mysteries and all knowledge, and though I have all faith, so that I could remove mountains, but have not love, I am nothing.
>
> —1 CORINTHIANS 13:1–2

Developing and creating new relationships is how most witnessing goes forward. Most unbelievers will trust believers they feel care about them. Usually witnessing is about developing short-term or long-term relationships. Winning souls is always bringing these relationships to salvation closure.

## Now Is Your Time to Learn to Win Souls

Believers should always look for opportunities to share the love of Jesus to a lost and dying world, to be available to help, serve and encourage unbelievers at any time. Of course, the greatest service to an unbeliever is to lead him or her to receive Jesus Christ as Savior—they will literally thank you for it!

For the last fifty years or so there has been general consensus in the body of Christ that approximately 90 percent of all believers have never won a soul to Jesus as Savior. This is a shocking statistic, which can and must be reversed. The exciting news is that with the *Witnessing Winzone* plan, millions of believers like you can now begin to help reverse these unbelievable numbers. This creative soulwinning plan will equip you to sensitively win unbelievers in such a way that lets them experience the love of Christ through you.

## Solving the
## Greatest Soulwinning Problems

When believers are one-on-one with unbelievers, regardless of their relationship or environment, they are faced with a basic witnessing challenge. This enormous challenge is complicated by the combination of *fear factors* resident in the believer: *What do I say now* or *What do I say next* or *What will they say and how do I answer?* The basic fear factor is from not knowing what to say or how to handle witnessing encounters. The combination of these two are the greatest obstacles to soulwinning for believers. Without understanding how to oversee witnessing exchanges and the direction in which to take them, there is always the lurking fear of what to say or do next. As a result of the fear factor, many believers freeze in their attempts to communicate the gospel; sadly, many have become resigned to doing absolutely nothing in that regard.

Caught in ignorance and fear, it is easy for some believers to convince themselves, *God just doesn't want me to witness*. The good news is that fear of witnessing can be completely eliminated by understanding what to do, when to do it, how to do it and where to do it. The solution to becoming an effective witness for Christ is to be willing to learn and to master the *Witnessing Winzone* plan because it will free you from these primary fear problems. It will take a small effort, but one that will be life changing. It was the apostle Paul who wrote,

> For God has not given us a spirit of fear, but of power and of love and of a sound mind.
>
> —2 TIMOTHY 1:7

## A REALISTIC
## PERSPECTIVE ABOUT WINNING SOULS

In approaching the goal of learning how to win souls, it is very realistic to realize that no believer is going to win to Jesus Christ every unsaved person they encounter. When equipped to win souls, believers do not live in doubt about themselves and what they can do in personal evangelism. They do not have to live with the former reality of being unprepared to deal with unbelievers. When a believer is equipped with this strategic soulwinning plan they can become a powerful and unstoppable soulwinner

However, believers will also have to learn to set aside unnecessary guilt that arises from the faulty thinking that Jesus expects you to win to the Lord every unsaved person you meet in life. Soulwinning success is an exciting experience and challenge. When a believer becomes completely equipped to win souls a new life and new attitude comes with that equipping. While it is also true that when believers learn this soulwinning plan, they begin winning more souls to Christ than they ever imagined, they must not be discouraged if they do not win all unbelievers they encounter.

The *Witnessing Winzone* plan will equip you so that you won't miss winning the unsaved that Jesus already has prepared for you to win. Learning to win souls using this plan is like learning to ride a bike. Once you learn how you will never forget.

After you are equipped to win souls you will begin to see soul-winning opportunities that you never realized existed. Unbelievers that the Holy Spirit has prepared to be won are gathered around every believer. Until believers are trained and become soulwin-ning minded, opportunities can easily slip away, completely unno-ticed. Through the *Witnessing Winzone plan* you will learn to not miss them and can win the souls that Jesus has already prepared for you to win.

Here are two key areas in personal evangelism that will take place for you. These are significant issues that you will quickly become victorious in with this easily learned soulwinning plan:

## #1: IMMEDIATELY PRODUCE SOULWINNING RESULTS

You may be surprised at your ease in leading unbelievers to Jesus Christ: when using the *Witnessing Winzone* strategy. It provides you with strategic questions to ask the unbeliever, using a very unique transition technique to a gospel presentation, giving spe-cific scriptures to quote before leading them in a prayer of faith. One of the most delicate challenges in witnessing is how to sensi-tively bring an unbeliever to an understanding of his or her spiri-tual condition and eternal danger. Believers can become successful in the witnessing process, and they will learn how to handle and deal with the following basic witnessing challenges:

- How to lead an unbeliever to an understanding of their spiritual and eternal danger in a loving, sensitive and acceptable manner.

- How to sensitively and effectively deal with statements such as: *I don't believe in God, Jesus, hell, heaven or the*

*Bible*, with instructions regarding how to overcome them and bring the person to salvation.

- How to present the Word of God in a way that unbelievers will see and understand their own spiritual need for salvation.

- How to gently guide unbelievers in a way that they will quickly trust in your leadership and allow you to lead them to receive Jesus Christ as Savior.

The scriptures teach that, as a believer, you should "always be ready to give a defense to everyone who asks you a reason for the hope that is in you, with meekness and fear" (1 Pet. 3:15). A tremendous point of assurance for believers is to understand that unsaved persons will not have an at-the-ready, on guard defense plan against the strategy in the *Witnessing Winzone* plan.

### You and the Unbeliever Enter the *Witnessing Winzone*

When athletes talk about having a great day in competition, they sometimes discuss that day in terms of being in a special *zone*. This *zone* speaks about a special sense of accomplishment on a performance day. This is a day when they know that everything that they attempt will work. They have a sense that they cannot be stopped; that nobody can touch them and everything that they do will be right. They don't *think* they are going to win the contest on that day—they *know* it! They know that they are having an incredible and perfect day when it is happening. When athletes are in a *zone* they have a unique sense of reality about themselves, the other participants, the environment and a sense that they will ultimately be victorious. That feeling transcends any normal levels of confidence. When these athletes talk about being in a *zone* they know it has all come together.

Believers equipped to win souls will enter a similar *zone*, in this case a *winzone*. They will have a unique sense of reality about themselves, about those to whom they are witnessing, and about their environment, along with a sense that they will be victorious. By introducing the *Witnessing Winzone* soulwinning plan to an unbeliever, you are also bringing them into the *winzone*. It has a beginning, a middle and closing. It is a place of safety and success for both the believer and unbeliever. Your success is winning an unsaved person to Christ; the success of the unsaved person, of course, is in receiving Christ. Everyone wins when a believer wins an unsaved person to Jesus as Savior! That is exactly what this soulwinning plan will do for you in personal evangelism and why it is named the *Witnessing Winzone*.

## REACH OUT WHERE YOU ARE

Are you aware that there are already unsaved people all around you ready to receive Christ? That God has prepared them for you to encounter them? Jesus and the Holy Spirit have already prepared untold numbers of unsaved persons everywhere in the world, in various cultures, to receive Him. Believers just need to be prepared to lead them to a point of accepting the Savior where and when they meet them.

The greatest basic need in personal evangelism is for believers to become well equipped to witness and win souls. In doing so, they have the ability to make adjustments in their message as needed and to win those who cross their paths no matter what the situation or circumstance. Unbelievers who are ready to be won to Christ can surface wherever believers happen to be at any given time. *This is the true mission field—a believer's immediate field of opportunity.* Unsaved people may be in desperate situations with circumstances beyond their own ability to remedy. The Lord knows about them and He knows about you. He can bring together a believer who can win an unbeliever who is ready to be won. It is important to understand that:

- Unbelievers have no idea God has prepared you to provide spiritual answers for their needs.

13

- Unbelievers have no idea that God has prepared them to receive spiritual answers for their needs.

- Neither believer nor unbeliever realizes that they have a divine appointment together. The Holy Spirit always finds the time and place for them to meet.

- Believers must be equipped and ready because these divine appointments can come at any time and place. Paul exhorted Timothy: Preach the word! Be ready in season and out of season. Convince, rebuke, exhort, and with all longsuffering and teaching (2 Tim. 4:2).

The Holy Spirit will use any life situation to prepare the hearts of unbelievers to be won to Christ. When you are equipped to win souls with the *Witnessing Winzone* plan and develop a soulwinning mindset, the Holy Spirit will prompt you when to speak. As you lead them step-by-step, you will bring them to a *teachable moment*, present the salvation gospel of Jesus Christ, and lead them through their salvation decision.

As you become equipped to win souls you will easily recognize the ready opportunities. These opportunities seem to come out of nowhere, but that is not the case. God has sent them to you. It is as simple as one, two, three, when you, the Holy Spirit, and the unbeliever meet together in a sacred appointment arranged by God. The scriptures declare:

> But the Helper, the Holy Spirit whom the Father will send in My name, He will teach you all things, and bring to your remembrance all things that I said to you.
>
> —JOHN 14:26

> However, when He, the Spirit of truth, has come, He will guide you into all truth; for He will not speak on His own authority, but whatever He hears he will speak; and He will tell you things to come.
>
> —JOHN 16:13

**Win Them! Invite Them!**

Instead of simply inviting unbelievers to church, win them to Christ first!

As you study and learn to use this plan, you will find that sometimes it is easier to win people to Christ than to successfully invite them to church. As you get equipped, you can win them and then invite them to your church or refer to them another Bible-believing church. Many people are only comfortable with the approach to evangelizing that simply invites someone to attend church. The basis of that kind of outreach invitation is to get them to church so that the pastor to win them to Christ. The reality is that as you learn to use the soulwinning plan you can win people to Christ as easily as you can invite them to church. Winning them is easier than actually getting them to visit a church.

It is wonderful to invite unbelievers to church, but how much more wonderful to experience the great joy and blessing of personally leading someone to receive Christ. Then when you bring them to church, they come with a whole new perspective of why they are there. They are now coming for the purpose of hearing more about Jesus Christ and being discipled and taught the Word of God to get their lives established on the solid foundation of biblical principles. Believers who know how to win souls can now invite newly won believers to church.

## #2: DON'T WORRY ABOUT GIFTS

You may ask, *Do I have to have a special gift for winning souls in personal evangelism?* Actually, what this questions refers to is the biblical reference to Christ giving gifts, as the apostle Paul declared: "And He Himself gave some to be apostles, some prophets, some *evangelists*, and some pastors and teachers" (Eph. 4:11emphasis mine). Theologians have come to call these gifts that Christ gave to the church *office gifts*. Some Christian leaders estimate that around 10 percent of the members of the body of Christ have a supernatural gift for evangelism. However, that is not the prerequisite for winning souls.

For Chrisitans who believe it is simply not their "gift" to witness and evangelize the lost, let me state clearly:

- You do not need to be especially gifted to win souls.

- You do not need to have special qualifications to be trained to win souls.

- You only need to be willing to learn how to win souls.

Jesus gave the Great Commission to *all* believers to witness and make disciples of all nations. These commands are not based upon receiving or demonstrating a spiritual gift; they are based upon obedience to Him. All believers are to witness in the co-shared mission of winning the world to Jesus. When believers witness to the unsaved they are obeying Christ's commands:

> Go therefore and make disciples of all the nations, baptizing them in the name of the Father and of the Son and of the Holy Spirit.
>
> —MATTHEW 28:19

> But you shall receive power when the Holy Spirit has come upon you; and you shall be witnesses to Me in Jerusalem, and in all Judea and Samaria, and to the end of the earth.
>
> —ACTS 1:8

### Gifted evangelists

Some believers, who have a special evangelistic gift, when asked how they win souls often respond by saying, "I don't know, I just do it." Their response, though honest, is not entirely true. It would be more accurate for them to say that they know what they are doing but cannot *articulate* how or what they are doing. They simply do not have a transferable or teachable model to share with other believers who desire to wins souls. However, at one time or another these gifted evangelists developed *a personal strategy—or witnessing technique*—for the purpose of winning souls. In their thinking they have identified a plan or system that they know by experience works for them; they simply do not know how to articulate that plan or witnessing concepts.

Perhaps through trial and error, these gifted believers developed their own personal strategy or technique to win souls. Their personal techniques are energized by their gifting and are usually quite simple. It is important to note that in witnessing and winning souls there is always a strategy at a fundamental level that makes a believer effective.

Years ago I knew an usher in my church who was a very effective soulwinner. He easily identified visitors attending the church service and almost every Sunday won a visitor to Christ. This senior citizen usher had developed a "church usher approach" to winning souls. He was fun to talk with about winning souls, but he could not explain how he did it. He too would say, "I don't know, I just do it!"

## Winning Souls is NOT out–talking unbelievers

Because these so-called gifted evangelists seem to win souls without an apparent "soulwinning technique," the fallacy has arisen in some believers' minds that these evangelists win souls by simply *outtalking unbelievers*. Since most believers feel they cannot do that, they feel intimidated by their gifted counterparts, and become discouraged in their efforts, thinking, *Why try?*. The reality is that probably many of these gifted soulwinners could be duplicated if they were able to articulate, analyze, and write their method for winning souls so that others could use their technique.

The goal is definitely not to learn how to *outtalk an unbeliever*. The objective is to learn how to lead unbelievers to accept the love of Jesus Christ and make Him their personal Savior. No believer can be taught to simply *outtalk an unbeliever*, but they can be taught how to lead an unbeliever to salvation with the soulwinning plan, and that is precisely what the *Witnessing Winzone* plan will do for you.

### Purpose for evangelism gift

Do not allow yourself to feel limited because of a misperception of the qualifications for winning souls. According to the scriptures, the main role of a gifted evangelist in the body of Christ (as with the other "office" gifts) is to equip believers like you to do the work of the evangelist:

> And He Himself gave some to be apostles, some prophets, some evangelists, and some pastors and teachers, for the equipping of the saints for the work of the ministry, for the edifying of the body of Christ, till we all come to the unity of the faith and of the knowledge of the Son of God, to a perfect man, to the measure of the stature of the fullness of Christ.
> —EPHESIANS 4:11–13

Not all believers are "gifted" to be evangelists, but all believers are called to be witnesses and to do the work of an evangelist: "But you be watchful in all things, endure afflictions, do the work of an evangelist, fulfill your ministry" (2 Tim. 4:5). Many church leaders agree that believers may have several giftings that blend together in useful ways to help in building the kingdom of God.

For example, if, after a believer hears a gifted teacher present a sermon in church, and he or she goes out and shares it with another person, is that not a kind of "teaching"? Are believers disqualified from teaching others because they may not have received the *spiritual gift* of teaching? When a believer shares the gospel with an unbeliever, are they not also teaching in the process of evangelizing? Pastors who have the spiritual gift of teaching are equipping those who hear them to teach others what they just taught them. In principle, the same is true of those believers who have the spiritual gift of an evangelist. Biblically, their purpose is to equip others to evangelize and win souls in the same way they have learned to do.

Those who are gifted as evangelists and walk in obedience to their calling can be very effective at personal evangelism. They are supposed to be effective; their gifting makes them so. For that same reason, they should be uniquely qualified to teach others how to evangelize. Those with the gift of evangelism are not to be considered a part of an elite group, while other believers stand around, watching in awe at what only these gifted evangelists can do.

Believers should never put themselves in a box of limitation concerning their abilities in personal evangelism. Nor should a believer allow anyone to tell them what they cannot achieve in winning souls. Any believer can be taught to win souls if they want to be taught. Occasionally you may come across someone who ridicules the idea of studying in preparation to win souls. So be aware, be wise and stay focused on getting equipped to do your own work in winning souls.

## SEVEN GOALS OF THE WITNESSING WINZONE

This book has several goals, with the primary goal being to teach you exactly how to immediately win souls and to give you a foundation to consistently win souls for the rest of your life. Once equipped with this plan, you will discover and understand the many dynamics and subtleties surrounding any type of witnessing and soulwinning exchange. You can adapt the *Witnessing Winzone* plan easily and quickly to your own personality and lifestyle. Learning to win souls is the basis of the other goals for this book, which will naturally fall into place as you embrace the primary goal. These other goals are not complicated, but are a part of helping you realize all your hopes and dreams for being effective in personal evangelism. Let me summarize briefly the seven goals of this book for making you an effective soulwinner.

### 1. Winning souls

The primary goal of this book for you to learn how to lead unsaved people to receive Jesus as Savior using the *Witnessing Winzone* plan. In accomplishing this goal you will develop a whole new perspective about what is called witnessing in personal evangelism. You will transition from having a limited concept of what witnessing can accomplish to the unlimited possibilities that await you when you master this soulwinning technique.

## 2. Reaping, not sowing

The second goal is to change your perspective from a *sowing* mindset into a *reaping* mindset. This may require an attitude change about witnessing in general and about sharing your personal testimony with unbelievers. You will develop a new mindset with the goal to actually win a soul to Jesus Christ, because you now know how. Your mindset will change from thinking, *I just want to sow a seed into an unsaved person's life and at the right time someone else will win them to Jesus Christ.* Instead you will think, *I know that I can win them to Jesus Christ.* You will develop a reaping mindset because you will know what to do yourself.

## 3. Balancing your perspective

The third goal is for you to understand the need to have a balanced perspective between reaping and sowing. After winning several people to Christ, you may develop the mindset that reaping is all you want to do, and settle for that as a personal goal. However, once you have the skills to win souls, you will quickly understand that as you go to reap you automatically sow. Reaping, not sowing, is the priority. As you have the right balanced perspective for personal evangelism, your sowing will become more focused.

## 4. Learning to "bring to salvation closure"

The fourth goal is for you to actually win souls to Christ, not limited to simply sharing your testimony or inviting unbelievers to church. This involves developing the attitude that "bringing to salvation closure" will become the goal in witnessing exchanges. You will develop a new, gentle tenacity as a result of having soulwinning closing skills. With the knowledge you will gain in this plan, you will not want to give up and will be undeterred in this goal. You will learn to handle different kinds of witnessing situations. Your mindset will always be to seek ways to bring soulwinning closings in witnessing because you now know you can.

### 5. Gaining confidence

The fifth goal is for you to have a confident mindset regarding your approach to personal evangelism. To be prepared, feel assured and alert to the reality that, at appropriate times, you will be equipped to act immediately and precisely. At times, your soulwinning timeframe with an unbeliever will be limited. You will be equipped to know how to strike while the iron is hot and quickly lead an unsaved person to a decision for Jesus Christ.

### 6. Developing consistency

The sixth goal is for you to become a consistent soulwinner and fully discover God's plan, purpose and will for your life. Once you learn to win souls, you can live a fulfilled life in Jesus Christ according to 2 Timothy 4:5: "do the work of the evangelist, fulfill your ministry." Scripture establishes a powerful and connective cord between doing the work of an evangelist and experiencing the full potential of a fulfilled life in Christ that He has for you.

### 7. Equipping others

The seventh goal is for you to become so equipped that you will be excited and be able to encourage, train, and equip others to win souls. You can become a resource for your church as one who can teach others how to win souls.

## UNBELIEVERS ARE WILLINGLY LED BY BELIEVERS

If you have never led an unbeliever to Christ and have concerns about doing so, you will now be able to lay your fears aside. It has been my experience that, most times, unbelievers are ready and willing to be led by believers in spiritual situations. They are often searching for things that will improve their lives. If handled right, they are more than willing to led to the greatest life improvement of all, salvation through Jesus Christ. Unbelievers usually have no problem listening to sensitive, caring believers and being led by them. It is when believers mishandle a witnessing exchange that the unbeliever receives validation for the negative perception of Christians today. Tragically, unbelievers then feel more secure about not responding to you and becoming a Christian or *religious person.*

Unbelievers want reasons to do or to not do things. If an unbeliever visits a church—and that might be once a year or once every two or three years—he or she is overtly giving permission to be led as soon as they enter the front door. Ushers tell them where to sit and the order of worship tells them when to stand, what to sing and how to do whatever goes on in the service. Most importantly, an unsaved visitor, just by being in a church service, has given the ministering speaker permission to present the gospel of Jesus Christ to them. An unsaved person in a church service is a captive audience; he has become willing to be in that kind of a controlled situation. Do not for a second think that unbelievers cannot be led. They can and are more than willing to be led in spiritual directions. It is just a question of who is going to lead them.

You are about to discover that in the midst of witnessing the *Witnessing Winzone* plan creates a unique situation very similar to a captive audience in a church service. The strategy in the plan leads an unbeliever to give that same kind of unspoken permission to have the salvation gospel presented to them. The Bible has always had a pattern and strategy for dealing with those who are unsaved or do not know about the things of God through Jesus Christ. It is this pattern and strategy that is the key to learning how to win souls for the rest of your life.

2

# The Biblical Strategy to Win Souls

U NLESS BELIEVERS ARE EQUIPPED WITH a clear and precise soulwinning plan, the evasive tactics of an unbeliever will frustrate practically every witness exchange. The *Witnessing Winzone* soulwinning plan is easily applied in any witness exchange and under any circumstance, condition or environment. From its beginning during my initial soulwinning experience at the 1984 Olympics, this strategy has been developed into a successful soulwinning plan for any situation. The uniqueness of the soulwinning plan is its biblical strategy, simplicity, readiness, and flexibility with which it can be applied.

## "HIDDEN" BIBLICAL STRATEGY IN PLAIN VIEW

The Bible records a specific strategy and pattern for dealing with individuals and winning unbelievers to Christ. It has always been there; it has just not been identified as a soulwinning strategy. The model and strategy for personal evangelism and soulwinning is illustrated in the account found in Acts 8:26–37, which records the story of Philip and the Ethiopian eunuch. It reveals a pattern model that involves *asking strategic questions* to create a teachable moment as an effective biblical strategy to witness to and win an unsaved person. Philip is the biblical role model of how to win souls through personal evangelism today.

23

Of course, Jesus Christ often employed the use of questions in His ministry to His disciples and to the multitudes. For example, when He knew it was time to reveal who He was to His disciples, He asked them the question, "Who do men say that I, the Son of Man, am?" (Matt. 16:13). And it was God the Father who was the first to initiate the practice of asking questions to lead people to truth, when He came into the garden looking for Adam and his wife and called to them, "Where are you?" (Gen. 3:9). Let's investigate each of these question-asking scenarios to see what we can learn from them for our purposes of personal evangelism.

## PHILIP'S SIMPLE APPROACH

The story of Philip and the Ethiopian eunuch is a fascinating story. It is the biblical model for teaching the body of Christ the value of asking thought-provoking questions as part of the strategy in witnessing and winning souls. As twenty-first century Christians, we can still identify with this biblical account of a believer confronting an unbeliever, because basic interactions between the saved and unsaved never change. The primary goal is always to win an unsaved person to Jesus Christ. Let's review the biblical account and learn to apply Philip's strategy for soulwinning today:

> Now an angel of the Lord spoke to Philip, saying, "Arise and go toward the south along the road which goes down from Jerusalem to Gaza." This is desert. So he arose and went. And behold, a man of Ethiopia, a eunuch of great authority under Candace the queen of the Ethiopians, who had charge of all her treasury, and had come to Jerusalem to worship, was returning. And sitting in his chariot, he was reading Isaiah the prophet. Then the Spirit said to Philip, "Go near and overtake this chariot."
>
> So Philip ran to him, and heard him reading the prophet Isaiah, and said, "Do you understand what you are reading?"

And he said, "How can I, unless someone guides me?" And he asked Philip to come up and sit with him. The place in the Scripture which he read was this:

"He was led as a sheep to the slaughter; And as a lamb before its shearer is silent, So He opened not His mouth. In His humiliation His justice was taken away, And who will declare His generation? For His life is taken from the earth."

So the eunuch answered Philip and said, "I ask you, of whom does the prophet say this, of himself or of some other man?" Then Philip opened his mouth, and beginning at this Scripture, preached Jesus to him. Now as they went down the road, they came to some water. And the eunuch said, "See, here is water. What hinders me from being baptized?"

Then Philip said, "If you believe with all your heart, you may."

And he answered and said, "I believe that Jesus Christ is the Son of God."

So he commanded the chariot to stand still. And both Philip and the eunuch went down into the water, and he baptized him. Now when they came up out of the water, the Spirit of the Lord caught Philip away, so that the eunuch saw him no more; and he went on his way rejoicing.

—ACTS 8:26–39

Philip's strategic soulwinning style is uncomplicated. His model of approaching the Ethiopian eunuch contains two simple elements that engage this stranger of another race and culture in a life-changing exchange.

### First element: stimulating receptivity

The first element is to stimulate an attitude of receptivity, a teachable moment, for the salvation gospel through the use of a *strategic question*. He simply asked the eunuch, "Do you understand what you are reading?" (Acts 8:30). The eunuch honestly admitted that he did not, and could not understand unless someone who did could lead him. He was interested in what he was reading, and wanted to understand it. That made him receptive to Philip's question. A vital key to winning souls is the ability to lead unbelievers into an attitude of receptivity that allows them to hear biblical answers to life-changing questions. This strategic approach in witnessing and winning souls is as valid today as it was in Philip's time.

When a believer wants to convince an unbeliever about receiving Christ as Savior, there are primarily two approaches. The first approach is ineffective, usually resulting in no decision for salvation. The second is what I have incorporated into this soulwinning strategy that leads to a soul won to Christ:

1. *Ineffective approach.* In many witnessing exchanges, believers impose ideas, concepts or life direction by simply beginning to tell a person about Jesus. At times believers try to tell unbelievers about a new life direction, whether the unsaved person listening is interested or not. Believers have been known to then elaborate or even argue the point with no specific conclusion as a goal.

2. *Effective approach.* To be effective in soulwinning, it is important to creatively stimulate a mental and emotional attitude of receptivity in an unbeliever toward salvation in Jesus Christ by asking unique questions. This strategy employs questions to draw out what an unbeliever thinks in a style and manner that can lead the unsaved person towards the specific goal of their receiving Jesus as Savior.

This biblical strategy helps believers to avoid saying too much about the wrong things, at the wrong time, and in the wrong way. They simply ask the unbeliever a question of significant interest. One of the fundamental problems in witnessing is that it sounds as if the would-be soulwinner is selling something. In the world of sales and marketing, *selling* is *telling*. No one likes to be told. Unbelievers especially do not like to feel they are being lectured to. Unbelievers don't want to be sold, they want to be led.

With no clear direction in a witness exchange, believers often hammer away and beat believers over the head with one Bible fact after another. Some witnessing exchanges I have observed, and at one time even participated in, are sort of like throwing mud against the wall to see if it will stick. All people, including unbelievers, enjoy talking about and listening to what they are interested in. This biblical strategy of asking strategic questions provokes and stimulates unbelievers to become interested in the subject at hand: their coming death and relationship with Jesus Christ.

### Second element: explanation and closing

When the eunuch had answered Philip's question, revealing his receptivity to hear this stranger who just appeared in the desert, Philip presents and explains the scriptures that he is reading to the eunuch. He then brings the witnessing exchange to a close by leading the eunuch to Jesus Christ as Savior.

Perhaps like you, I don't know how many times over the years I have read this exciting story. Most believers have probably read it many times. I believe this subtle but extremely powerful soulwinning strategy has been overshadowed by the supernatural events of the text. The witnessing model has been overlooked because of the more exciting and miraculous event of Philip being caught away at the end of his experience with the eunuch: "...the Spirit of the Lord caught Philip away, so that the eunuch saw him no more; and he went on his way rejoicing" (Acts 8:39).

Some have treated this account as if the eunuch accepting Christ was a peripheral story, simply a background to set the stage for the more exciting and miraculous event of Philip being caught away. However wonderful it is to see men and women supernaturally touched by the Holy Spirit in incredible ways, we need to recognize that this text has more to teach us. At some point I recognized that it is a biblical model for winning souls as well. I saw an intentional, divine strategy for dealing with an unsaved person, no matter who they are in life or where they happen to be located at the moment.

### Philip's strategy works today.

This biblical soulwinning strategy works for witnessing exchanges today almost identically to the way Philip led the eunuch to accept Jesus as Savior. The strategy is the same and the circumstances and players in the story could be played out in any community in the world today. The only basic differences are that the names are changed and the strategic questions may be different today. In our present day, just as in Philip's day, unbelievers turn up in the most unexpected places and situations. In all of scripture, there is no other illustration of a soulwinning scenario similar to what believers face in the twenty-first century or any other century.

Let's observe Philip's attitude, his pattern of speaking, and the wonderful results he realized in dealing with the witnessing challenge before him. It may surprise you how quickly you will recognize the similarity of the situation to what any believer can face today in daily witnessing opportunities. I have found it fascinating to relate to Philip's ease of soulwinning during his lifetime and then to realize the same strategy that worked for him works for us today. Let's consider the elements of his success.

### Philip was sensitive to the Holy Spirit.

Philip was sensitive to hearing from the Holy Spirit's leading. Notice that Philip did not argue or look for an excuse for not making the long trip into the desert because witnessing in this type situation might be inconvenient. Where the Lord led, Philip followed. Philip was not afraid to deal with an unusual situation because he was confident that the Holy Spirit was leading him and would give him help to handle any situation. Philip dealt with the situation as it was. He did not have pre-conceived ideas or make demands that he would witness only under conditions that were convenient or comfortable for him.

### Philip was obedient to the Holy Spirit.

Not only did Philip hear and obey the voice of the Spirit to go to the desert, but he was obedient to approach the chariot of this Ethiopian eunuch. The chariot would have made a distinctive statement of the eunuch's high position, authority and power in a foreign nation. In fact, the eunuch was the treasurer for the

Queen of Ethiopia. There were probably aides, a driver or other personnel around the eunuch. Philip was from another culture and probably a lower economic and social class. In the world the eunuch was a very successful person, notwithstanding his being a eunuch. Yet, Philip was not intimidated because he knew how to handle himself in a witnessing and soulwinning exchange. And it is obvious from the text that the eunuch did not object when Philip approached him.

**Philip was not put off by the circumstances.**

Philip's goal was not to invite the eunuch to a church service in order to have someone else try to win him to Christ. The eunuch did not have to be in a "normal" place like a temple, a church or a residence to engage in a witnessing exchange. Philip understood that a believer must be willing to win an unbeliever to Christ, no matter the circumstances that present the opportunity for a witnessing exchange.

**Philip asked a strategic question.**

Philip did not approach the eunuch to tell him how much he loved Jesus or how much Jesus meant to his own life. He did not begin a conversation sharing self-focused testimony about how Jesus changed his life. Rather, he projected himself into the circumstances of the eunuch, observing that he was reading the scriptures.

- Philip simply asked the eunuch a question: *Do you understand what you are reading?* Perhaps his question followed a brief, friendly greeting, but what is significant is that Philip immediately and gently took charge of the conversation with the eunuch through the use of a strategic question. That question caused the eunuch to start thinking about what he did not understand. Through his question, Philip was able to lead the eunuch to a teachable moment.

- It was his strategic question that opened the door for Philip to present the Word of God to the eunuch. As

Philip proceeded to present Jesus Christ from the scriptures the eunuch was reading, the power of God touched
the eunuch. And Philip easily led the eunuch to his decision to receive Jesus as Savior.

- It is important to note that Philip was focused. He had a
  goal to win the eunuch to Christ. Philip was a reaper and
  had a reaper's mindset, because he knew he could win the
  eunuch. Philip was not intimidated by his position as the
  Treasurer of the Queen of Ethiopia; he only saw a man.
  Philip had been obedient to the voice of the Spirit, which
  led him to an unsaved person to whom he knew he was to
  witness. And he was not intimidated or confused by the
  eunuch's cultural, political or economic status. He simply
  considered his need to know Christ.

- Philip used his strategic question to bring the eunuch
  to a teachable and receptive moment to listen to what
  Philip had to say. This caused the eunuch to want Philip
  to explain the answer and Philip used the opportunity to
  preach Jesus Christ. That is the value of using a strategic
  question: to cause an unsaved person to want to hear
  more about what they do not understand. The more they
  want to hear, the more they will give you the opportunity to present Jesus Christ as Savior. It is this wisdom to
  which Christ referred when he declared, "Behold, I send
  you out as sheep in the midst of wolves. Therefore be wise
  as serpents and harmless as doves" (Matt. 10:16)

The lesson for believers today is that Philip could lead and
win the eunuch because he understood how to handle a witness
exchange and win someone to Christ. The general circumstances
in which believers in the twenty-first century find themselves are
really no different. For the most part believers will be led to win
unsaved people in work areas, family situations, in social settings
and sometimes to an occasional stranger in normal places like
planes, trains, offices or parking lots. Equipped with the *Witnessing*

*Winzone* plan, you, like Philip, will be prepared to quickly win an unsaved person to Christ, under any situation you can imagine.

## JESUS USED STRATEGIC QUESTIONS

In Matthew 16:13–16, when Jesus knew that it was the time for the truth to be revealed concerning who He is, He asked two simple, but very strategic questions:

> When Jesus came into the region of Caesarea Philippi, He asked His disciples, saying, "Who do men say that I, the Son of Man, am?" So they said, "Some say John the Baptist, some Elijah, and others Jeremiah or one of the prophets." He said to them, "But who do you say that I am?" Simon Peter answered and said, "You are the Christ, the Son of the living God."

First, Jesus asked a strategic question about the general population's belief as to who they think He is: *"Who do men say that I, the Son of Man, am?"* His first question prepared them up for the second question. Their initial answer was to give Him rumor information: *"Some say John the Baptist, some Elijah, and others Jeremiah or one of the prophets."* It is important to note that as the disciples answered, Jesus did not demean or make fun of the answer. As others were named, Jesus did not overreact and try to defend Himself against the incorrect answers. What Jesus did was to ignore the incorrect answers. This is a vital point to grasp. He patiently let them answer based upon what they understood. Jesus ignored the incorrect answers and kept moving forward with what He wanted to accomplish in the conversation. In asking that first question, He assumed the leadership role. He took charge of whatever conversation would follow. Jesus asked a strategic question that would cause the disciples to respond and seriously think about who He was.

Secondly, Jesus directed the next question to the disciples, asking them who they thought He was: *But who do you say that I am?* Jesus, through His questions, was preparing the disciples to become receptive. He wanted them to hear and receive the

31

truth about Himself. Perhaps there was some sort of pause. Maybe the disciples looked around at each other uncertain as to how to answer the Master's question. But Peter was about to answer the question correctly, as the Spirit led him: *You are the Christ, the Son of the living God.* (vs.16)

**Jesus did not tell them; He prepared them to *hear*.**

It is important to understand that Jesus prepared the disciples to become receptive to hear the answer to His question, rather than declaring facts. He initiated a strategy that created what I refer to as a *teachable moment*. That is different from just telling people a fact without preparing them to receive it. This strategy makes all the difference in the world when witnessing the truths of the kingdom. Jesus and Philip both used the same strategy. Their conversations were different, but their strategy was exactly the same. As a result of Jesus asking the disciples strategic questions, they were prepared to wait for an answer—an answer that they wanted to hear. Through the strategy of asking a question they would not be sure of answering, they were led to become receptive to the answer. In this state of receptivity, waiting for the right answer, they were available to and willing to receive the truth of who He is.

Jesus could have simply told them, *Men gather around, I have an announcement about who I am. Don't listen to rumors. I am the Christ, the Son of the living God.* Instead, He prepared the disciples to receive the truth by strategically preparing them to hear it through the use of strategic questions. You may ask, *Did Jesus ask those questions as a strategy or was He merely asking questions out of curiosity?* I believe Jesus asked those questions for a specific reason: to prepare His disciples to receive the truth of Who He is. Jesus always knew what He was doing and how others would react to what He was doing and saying. Jesus knew that as He prepared the disciples to hear, the Holy Spirit would minister the truth to them regarding Who He is. By asking those questions, Jesus created a sense of receptivity and anticipation, eliminating any defensiveness, which leads to doubt and not being teachable. He created a teachable moment.

> For if our heart condemns us, God is greater than our heart, and knows all things.
>
> — 1 JOHN 3:20

Can you understand how different it is to prepare an unbeliever to receive answers or information, rather than a believer declaring statements of fact and imposing information upon an unbeliever?

## JESUS' TEACHING AND PARABLES STARTED WITH QUESTIONS

Jesus began many of His parables by first setting up what He wanted to say by asking a question of His audience. He strategically prepared people to become receptive to what He had to say. Jesus understood the power of questions and consistently used this tactic. He effectively used questions in His teaching and the strategy of asking key questions is built into the *Witnessing Winzone* soul-winning plan. One interesting example is found in Mark 11:28–33 when the chief priests, the scribes, and the elders came to Him to question His authority:

> And they said to Him, "By what authority are You doing these things? And who gave You this authority to do these things?" But Jesus answered and said to them, "I also will ask you one question; then answer Me, and I will tell you by what authority I do these things: The baptism of John—was it from heaven or from men? Answer me." And they reasoned among themselves, saying, "If we say, 'From men'"— they feared the people, for all counted John to have been a prophet indeed. So they answered and said to Jesus, "We do not know." And Jesus answered and said to them, "Neither will I tell you by what authority I do these things."

These were the most powerful religious leaders of the time and would have been quite intimidating. Jesus totally diffused and reversed their attack with the tactic of asking them a strategic question and in doing so maintained control of the conversation. He ultimately ended the conversation on His terms, not theirs. Throughout His ministry Jesus consistently handled a variety of challenging situations by employing the tactic of asking questions to lead to the conclusions He desired.

## ESTABLISHING A PATTERN IN THE BEGINNING

In the Garden of Eden, Adam and Eve fell into sin, choosing to disobey the commands of God. Their sinless, divine relationship with the Lord God was broken because of their sin. Yet, the Lord God, out of His love for His creation, immediately reached out to them to attempt to bring reconciliation. It is significant that He made strategic use of a question in His first attempt to reach fallen mankind. He did not begin by lecturing or condemning Adam and Eve. He did not criticize Adam, talk down to him or make a negative statement to him. When the Lord God wanted to initiate reconciliation, He simply asked Adam a question: "Where are you?" His response to their sin was to initiate reconciliation by asking questions they would have to answer. First, he asked Adam a strategic question:

> And they heard the sound of the Lord God walking in the garden in the cool of the day, and Adam and his wife hid themselves from the presence of the Lord God among the trees of the garden. Then the Lord God called to Adam and said to him, "Where are you?"
>
> —GENESIS 3:8–9

The strategy in God's question was to cause Adam to give an account to a very difficult subject. Why had he changed his behavior in the presence of God? Whey was he hiding from him? Having to answer for himself on such a critical issue led Adam to recognize his responsibility before a loving God. The Lord God's approach to

Adam is in sharp contrast to approaching unbelievers, or anyone for that matter, with attacks of criticism and condemnation for what they are doing. A thoughtless strategy of attacking, criticizing or condemning provokes people into becoming defensive and unteachable. The Lord God established a pattern of dealing with the first sinners by using a strategic question to create a teachable moment. The question He asked Adam opened a conversation that pointed to God's reconciling work through the ages, culminating in the redemptive work of Jesus Christ. Philip and Jesus used the same approach of asking questions as the Lord God did, and you can do this also as you employ the strategy of the *Witnessing Winzone*.

## SOCRATES 469–399 B.C.

Socrates was known as a great teacher. He had a commitment to truth as he knew it and set the standard for Western philosophy. He created the practice of philosophical discussion through the tactic of asking questions. His audience and students were primarily the wealthy young aristocrats of Athens. He constantly questioned their opinions of events and themselves. He was established as a great teacher because of his teaching style. It was by asking strategic questions to challenge his students' beliefs that he prepared them to be lead to the conclusions he wanted. In many colleges and universities today professors employ a Socratic approach to teaching.

## CONTROLLED DIRECTION

This biblical plan for witnessing and winning souls revolves around initially asking strategic questions. It was intentionally designed for believers to assert gentle leadership and gain control of the conversation. Of course, this reference to *control* is in the context of being in full partnership with the Holy Spirit. You will absolutely know when the moment is right to win an unbeliever. It is important for believers to be ready and have a sense of authority when the Holy Spirit is ready to work in an unbeliever's heart.

This kind of control comes when a believer knows what they are doing and can maintain the direction of the witness exchange. This soulwinning plan gives believers the ability to be ready at all times to assert leadership of witnessing exchanges.

It is important to note that this control is not for domination, but for maintaining the witnessing direction in order to lead an unbeliever to their decision to accept Jesus Christ as Savior. This controlled direction is to help prevent both believers and unbelievers from getting lost in unstructured dialogues. It is also to have a direction focus to bring witnessing conversations back on track if sidetracked for any reason. This plan gives believers the ability to take charge and maintain the direction and control of any witnessing exchange. This is your personal soulwinning strategy when you want to transition from general witnessing to actually leading an unbeliever to Christ.

- The overall strategy is for you to initiate a fresh direction in the witnessing conversation by introducing the *Witnessing Winzone* soulwinning plan, which is designed for believers to effectively present the salvation gospel of Jesus Christ through three short scriptures. The strategy is to create a teachable moment in the mind of an unbeliever through the use of a simple statement, a simple question, another statement of agreement that is recognized by all and a penetrating question about the eventual death of an unbeliever. These statements and questions bring an unbeliever to want to hear correct answers to deep and penetrating questions about their own eternal destiny.

- The direction change leads the unsaved person to a personal awareness of great eternal danger. The strategy is to raise the issue of the unsaved person's coming death and lead them into the position of explaining how they intend to deal with and face their own eternal death issues. Unbelievers always have difficulty doing that. This will take them to a place of uncertainty about their coming death and will stimulate an attitude of receptivity for answers about what they face in eternity. This simple strategy always leads to a teachable moment for unbelievers.

- There is a unique and simple transition from the unsaved person's response that gives believers the opportunity to present three short scriptures. This unique transition technique anticipates answers from unbelievers such as "I don't believe in God, Jesus, Heaven or hell." Through the strategy in the *Witnessing Winzone* believers learn to easily handle and deflect any answer that unbelievers want to state about what they believe. These scriptures are the clear presentation of the salvation gospel of Jesus Christ that believers can quickly learn to present. The scriptures with their interpretation are easily understood and received by unbelievers and are ultimately used to lead unbelievers to their salvation.

- The soulwinning plan ends at the conclusion of the presentation of the three short scriptures, after which a believer can easily lead an unbeliever in a prayer to receive Jesus As Savior.

When you introduce the subject of eternal life, you are clearly changing the direction of the conversation. You could have been discussing anything to that point. You could have discovered certain problems that the unsaved person is going through. It does not matter if there is as deep relationship with the unbeliever or a casual relationship. Keep in mind that you are credible because you are a Christian and far more credible than you may think. Believers who identify themselves as Christians and behave in caring, helpful ways will always be credible.

An unsaved person is always curious about you as a Christian and what you may have to say to them. They sense that you understand or have something that they do not. Therefore, they will be open to you and they will be easily led to Jesus using this simple strategy. Believers are like a living Bible. For certain unbelievers, you may be the only Bible those unbelievers have ever read. The apostle Paul calls believers *epistles* in 2 Corinthians 3:2: "You are our epistle written in our hearts, known and read by all men." Unbelievers will respond to believers because of the presence of Christ in the believers. And unbelievers will respond to the sensitive leadership of the believer.

## THE WITNESSING WINZONE SOULWINNING MODEL

As an illustration scenario, imagine being at a picnic. You may be anywhere, perhaps at a company picnic, where people are relaxed and having a comfortable day together. You could have previously been or now be newly sharing and witnessing to an unbeliever about the things of God in a general way. At a certain time, you sense that this is the day and time to win that unsaved person to Jesus Christ. When that occurs, a good option is to gently suggest that you and the unsaved person take a walk together. In doing so, you have initiated an environment change where you will not be disturbed. That is a simple step in taking charge. It is just using a little common sense. It does not matter where you are with an unbeliever: an office, parking lot, restaurant, etc. Just make sure that you have a sense that you will not be interrupted—that is taking control of the situation. If you and an unbeliever are in any crowded environment and if it is appropriate, simply suggest a walk to any private area.

In almost all real life situations, no matter where you are, leading an unbeliever to Jesus Christ as Savior will happen according to the model presented here. In the next chapter you will be presented with a broad explanation and analysis regarding what is taking place as you win an unsaved person to Christ. Read through the complete model sequence and try to avoid making judgments as you are going through the first time. I have given you a lot of information leading up to the actual *Witnessing Win-*

*zone* model to provide insight about the soulwinning process. You will have many questions answered as you also go through the analysis section after the conclusion of the model.

The analysis is a broader, indepth explanation of what takes place when the soulwinning plan is actually being implemented. The most important thing for you to understand at this point is that the results from implementing this soulwinning plan are phenomenal. It works and wins souls to Christ.

Although the *Witnessing Winzone* plan is divided into questions, statements, and scriptures, they are all one continuous flow of presentation. In presenting the model, I will use the name *Joe* for the unbeliever. Remember how Philip asked the eunuch, *Do you understand what you are reading?* Then he presented scriptures and led the eunuch to Jesus. The same method of asking a strategic question takes place here: When you sense the appropriate time to win the unbeliever and transition into the *Witnessing Winzone* strategy, begin with an easy speaking pace and a calm, caring voice. The following are examples of making that transition.

### Section 1. Transitional statements and questions

> YOU SAY: *"Joe, I talk to a lot of people about Jesus Christ, salvation and eternal life. May I ask you a question without being too personal?"*

They will normally give a quick OK; just immediately keep going.

> YOU SAY: *"We are all going to die someday, right?"*

Again wait for their response; it's always yes. Sometimes an unsaved person will look at you with a sort of "deer in the headlight" look. If they do then say, "I mean, physically we are all going to die, right?" This statement always brings them into reality and they will answer yes.

> YOU SAY: *"Let me ask you this Joe. When you die and it's time for you to go to heaven and Jesus Christ asks you, 'Joe, why should I let you into heaven and give you eternal life?' what would you say to Jesus?"*

This is their death and eternal danger question. Say nothing! Do not try to help them. They may struggle for an answer. Let them answer on their own. It is a discovery question to find out what they think and know about eternal issues. How they answer will reveal much about what they believe and it is a vital step in their preparation to be led to Christ.

At this point they might say anything. Most of the time their response will be something like: "I've tried to be a good person or I've tried to live a good life." No matter what they say, do not challenge it. Go immediately to the next step. Mirror back to them what they just said and put it in the context that what they said is normal. No matter what they said, it is normal to them and everyone likes to be told that they are normal. You are being sensitive and accommodating, not confronting in a negative way.

An unbeliever may respond and say, "I don't believe in Jesus" or "I don't believe in the Bible, heaven, or hell." The same principle applies—do not challenge them. They are not saved at this moment. That is why they do not believe in God, Jesus, the Bible, heaven, or hell. Do not be distracted by their statements, keep going; the goal is to get them saved, not get into arguments about religion. It does not matter what they say here. Your response is always the same—to transition or bridge into the gospel presentation.

> YOU SAY: *"That's a normal response; many people feel that way. I think most of us want to think we have tried to live a good life. Joe, let me share something with you that the Bible says about that for you, today."*

Do not hesitate; immediately go on to the next step, which is the three short scriptures. The unbeliever has been led to a place of considering their eternal danger and cannot answer correctly—and they know it. They will also know that you know that what they just answered is something they think you want to hear. The goal of the initial statements and questions is to prepare them for what is about to happen, the presentation of the salvation gospel of Jesus Christ through three short scriptures. This is a transitional response that will satisfy an unbeliever and allow you to maintain control of the presentation flow and immediately begin to present the Word of God to the unbeliever. They will want to hear what the Word of God has to say for them.

Through the strategic statements and questions, you led an unbeliever to a place of danger and vulnerability. You also led them into a teachable moment. You now will begin to lead them through three short scriptures to reveal the extent of their real danger. Then you will lead them into eternal safety and closure by receiving Jesus as Savior. Keep going through all three verses. Quote and explain all three verses as if they were one.

## Section 2. Three scriptures and closing prayer

> YOU SAY: *"Joe, in Romans 3:23 the Bible says, 'For all have sinned and come short of the glory of God.' Joe, that is a reference back to when Adam and Eve were in the Garden of Eden. God told them that they could have dominion over everything in the garden. Just don't do one thing, don't eat of the fruit of the tree of the knowledge of good and evil, or they would surely die. That's the old apple story!"*

Everyone is familiar with the story and when you include the reference to the "old apple story" they always nod in agreement.

41

"Adam and Eve ate of the fruit and that act of disobedience brought sin into the world and separated mankind from God spiritually for all eternity. Joe, when the Bible talks about death, unless it refers to a specific physical death, it is talking about spiritual death. Joe, as a result of that original sin in the Garden of Eden, we are all born spiritually separated from God."

YOU CONTINUE: "Joe, in Romans 6:23 the Bible says, 'For the wages of sin is death.' Joe, just like we receive wages for the work that we do, because of that original sin, we receive the wages of a spiritual death."

"Joe, people who are living and don't know God, in their heart know that they really do not know God. [Gesture toward their heart as you say this.] When they die, because they didn't know God in this life, they won't know God in eternal life. This is when the issue of heaven and hell comes up."

"Joe, the second half of that scripture says 'but the gift of God is eternal life through Jesus Christ our Lord.' What that means is that when Jesus was here on the earth, He went to the cross and took upon Himself the sin of the world. He died, was buried, and on the third day He arose from the dead and later ascended to Heaven. Joe, if we accept Jesus' sacrifice on the cross for our own sins, our sins are forgiven, and when we die we can have eternal life in Heaven."

> YOU CONTINUE: *"Joe, in Romans 10:9 the Bible says, 'If you confess with your mouth the Lord Jesus and believe in your heart that God has raised Him from the dead, you will be saved.' Joe, when the Bible talks about being saved, it means you must be saved from something; you are saved from going to hell and saved from living this life separated from God."*
>
> YOU SAY: *"Let me ask you this, Joe. Would you like to know that you can have eternal life in heaven someday?"*

Wait for their yes answer; it will come.

> *"Okay Joe, I'd like to lead you in a short prayer. This will be your prayer. We are going to invite Jesus Christ to be your Savior, forgive you of your sins, and give you eternal life. I will lead the prayer. You just repeat the prayer. Will you pray with me?"*

Wait for their yes answer; it will come.

> YOU SAY: *"Joe, this is your prayer. I will lead the prayer; you repeat the prayer: 'Heavenly Father, I accept Jesus Christ as my Savior. I ask you to forgive me of my sins and give me eternal life, and I will seek your will for my life. In Jesus' name I pray. Amen.'"*

The *Witnessing Winzone* Works!

That's it! It's that fast! You just led Joe to the Lord. Most of the time winning an unsaved to Christ will happen almost exactly as you saw it here. The impact of the Word of God upon a receptive, unsaved person is powerful and will greatly impact and transform them, as the scriptures declare:

> For the Word of God is quick, and powerful, and sharper than any twoedged sword, piercing even to the dividing asunder of soul and spirit, and of the joints and marrow, and is a discerner of the thoughts and intents of the heart.
>
> —Hebrews 4:12, kjv

The significant factor of this soulwinning plan is that it is clear, specific and flexible enough to quickly adapt to virtually any witnessing circumstance. You will quickly discover that it does not take the presentation of ten to fifteen Bible verses to win an unsaved person to Jesus Christ as Savior. This witnessing strategy strategically uses only three short scriptures with their interpretation and is completed in just a few minutes. These scriptures tell unbelievers all they need to know to receive Jesus Christ. In the world of sales and marketing there is an acrostic called "KISS." It stands for "Keep It Simple, Stupid!" I would never say that. I prefer "Keep It Simple, Saints!" As I was introduced at an evangelism seminar at Hoolywood Presbyterian Church in Hollywood, California, years ago, the Pastor of Evangelism said, "This is the simplest and most uncomplicated plan to win souls that I have ever seen. It is easy to learn and easy to present." The key in witnessing and winning souls is to keep things simple for both believers and unbelievers. The emphasis is strategically presenting the Word of God in a way that unbelievers can receive it. Because you, the witnessing believer, created a teachable moment, the unbeliever was ready to receive the Word of God. It does not take a theological lecture or argument to win an unsaved person to Christ.

Many times after I lead an unbeliever to their decision to receive Jesus as Savior, I pray for them. I ask their permission to pray a blessing upon them. I have never been refused and neither will you if you choose to ask. My prayer is generally like the following: *Heavenly Father, thank you for Joe and that today Joe's sins are forgiven and that Joe will have eternal life in heaven. I ask you to bless*

*Joe and bless Joe's family. Help Joe in all of his needs. In Jesus name I pray, Amen.* This is optional, but I personally believe a follow up prayer ministers to the new believer in a special way. I then direct them to a church fellowship that I feel is appropriate.

# 3

# The *Witnessing Winzone* Analysis

THE STRATEGY IN THE *Witnessing Winzone* soulwinning plan gives it precision, a fast track that is solid and uncomplicated. It works just as you read in the last chapter almost every single time. This witnessing model is divided into two functioning parts separated by a transition statement. Let's consider the simple steps that you just studied in the model and analyze their function.

## FUNCTION OF PART #1

The function of the first part is to create a teachable moment in the mind of an unbeliever. This is done by directing the witnessing conversation to the subject of death. A discovery question is asked to find out what an unsaved person thinks about their coming death. It is intended to draw out their thoughts about the all important subject of their death, beyond a basic yes or no type answer.

This penetrating question concerning death brings unbelievers to a receptivity of what you have to say and to a teachable moment. Unbelievers are rarely prepared to deal with this profoundly penetrating question, though they immediately realize its significance. Their responses are usually halfhearted and weak. The tenor of their responses may be flowery and self- serving, but they are generally not convincing. Unbelievers usually respond without a strong sense of conviction that they believe what they are say-ing. Their responses are more of a hope that maybe what they are saying is correct and that you will believe and accept their answer. They seem to know that they have missed it. The more they talk at this point, the more they realize what they do not understand. In that manner, a teachable moment is created. In spite of them-selves, they seem to invite your understanding of a subject they realize they do not have adequate answers for.

So by making some statements and asking some strategic ques-tions, you lead the unsaved person you are witnessing to into a place of concern about their coming death and eternal security. Before the main eternal danger question is asked, their thinking is being directed to the issue of death. In the following examples, a vague reference, a general reference and a direct reference to the eventual death of an unbeliever guide his thinking to the topic. This is a gentle, yet powerful way to introduce the subject of death and, in particular, the coming death of an unbeliever:

1. *I talk to a lot of people about Jesus Christ, salvation and eter-nal life.* This statement is a *vague* reference to death. At the same time it gives credibility, because you are stating that you talk to a lot of people about these subjects. The implication is that you know what you are talking about.

2. *May I ask you a question with out being to personal?* This is a simple and polite way to ask permission to engage and continue in a deeper conversation.

3. The agreeing statement, *We are all going to die someday, right?* is a *general* reference to death that all recognize as true.

4. The death and eternal danger question, *Let me ask you this Joe, When you die and it's time for you to go to heaven and Jesus Christ asks you, 'Joe why should I let you into heaven and give you eternal life?' What would you say to Jesus?* is a

*direct* reference to the future death of the unsaved person. It is a deep, powerful and penetrating question that an unbeliever will be unsure of how to answer, which opens them to receiving the right answer. This is a discovery question to draw out of an unbeliever more than a standard yes or no type answer. You will discover and understand a great deal about the unbeliever from this question. The unbeliever will also discover and understand a great deal about themselves from trying to answer it. This is a part of the process of creating the teachable moment.

As gentle and non-threatening as these questions are, an unbeliever will be totally unprepared for this sequence of thought provoking death references leading to a direct question about their own death. They are being led step by step into the thinking about the reality of their coming death. Most people are aware of the subject of death and can easily refer to the death of others. The unsaved will be inwardly shocked and unnerved when the subject of their own death is raised in such a direct manner. Perhaps for the first time someone that they are trusting, even if a new acquaintance, has confronted them in a gentle way about their future death. Unbelievers realize that suddenly they are in the midst of a very significant conversation about themselves and their own future—life after death. It has been my experience that approaching unbelievers in this way makes them want to know where the conversation will lead and how it will end.

Consider the seven direct references to the unbeliever in the discovery question:

> Let me **ask you this Joe**, "**When you die** and it's **time for you** to go to heaven and **Jesus Christ asks you**, 'Joe why should **I let you** into heaven **and give you** eternal life?' **what would you say** to Jesus?"

This discovery question about the death of an unbeliever is powerful, deep, penetrating and scary; it will give you their undivided attention. The death and eternal danger question is for believers to discover what an unbeliever thinks about this most personal subject. It is also for unbelievers to discover what they do not know about themselves. Most of the time unbelievers do not want you to know what they think or what is on their mind. As a general rule in witnessing encounters most unbelievers prefer to be vague and noncommital. By drawing out their answer you have led them to a place of personal vulnerability. They must expose part of their belief system. Through the strategic statement and question sequence you have led an unbeliever to expose what they think about the most significant question in life. In a courtroom when a witness inadvertantly reveals something about what they think, attorneys catagorize that type answer as *a bell that cannot be unrung*. From their response much can be understood about the unbeliever to whom you are witnessing. For example:

- Is the person unsaved or not? Any answer other than acknowledging that Jesus Christ is their Savior or a close variation of that is a strong indicator that the person is unsaved.

- Their answer brings to the *surface what they know or don't know* about the eternal death issue that they face. The unsaved will know that their answer is something that they think sounds good. They hope it sounds good to you. The unsaved person *will realize that you know what he or she does not know about this subject*.

- Unbelievers are immediately aware *of what they do not know* and understand about the eternal death issues. They have revealed their inability to give a good or right answer. Their lack of understanding and knowledge about the eternal death issue is now exposed. *They know that they don't know the answer*. They know that you know that they don't know the right answer. They will be *responsive to your leadership*.

49

- They *realize that they probably do not know or have a right answer* and that *you do know the right answer.* They will also realize that you know that they do not know what is right. They will become teachable and *receptive to you and your leadership* in providing the right answer.

- Your authority is being established and this opens the door for them to *submit to your gentle authority* and *leadership.* The unsaved have been led to a place of receptivity and will await your presentation and *leadership* in leading them out of their place of vulnerability.

- The unsaved *know that you have the answer.* They will absolutely give you the time to give it. They may not show it, but their interest in your answer will be high. This is a very sensitive and scary subject for an unbeliever. You will not see it, but spiritually, their knees are beginning to buckle!

- They know that you are handling this exchange in a good way. Their respect for you is solidifying because of how you are dealing with them on this most sensitive subject, their own death. They will respond in a good and positive way to your leading them through to the end of the gospel presentation.

The subject of an unbeliever's specific death was introduced in a low key and acceptable manner. This way of raising the death issue is one that both you and the unsaved person can feel comfortable with and participate in together. Because of the sensitivity in asking about the eternal questions in this form, you will have acceptability and credibility. When the strategic question, *When you die and its time for you to go to heaven . . .* is asked in this manner, it does not sound manipulative or unreal, because it is realistic and credible. Everyone accepts the reality that someday they will die. That is why the death and eternal danger question is based on a "when you die" context.

## TRANSITION STATEMENT:
## "THAT'S A NORMAL RESPONSE."

The function of the transition statement is to create a bridge between whatever an unbeliever has answered to your discovery question (and they can say anything) and the second functioning part of the model, which is the presentation of the Word of God.

No matter how they answer the "when you die" question, your response must be something like:

> That's a normal response; many people feel that way. I think most of us want to think we have tried to live a good life. Joe, let me share something with you that the Bible says about that for you, today.

This is an example of a transitional or bridge statement. The statement is designed to anticipate any answer from an unbeliever. Responding this way further builds your personal credibility as a sensitive and caring Christian person. In a very diplomatic style you are moving past whatever the unbeliever said. You are not demeaning the unbeliever or demeaning the unbeliever's answer. You are acknowledging their response and affirming their right to say it, in order to lead into the presentation of the salvation gospel of Jesus Christ. This is a tender moment and this gentle transition opens the way for you to clearly present the right answer found in the Word of God—and win them to Christ. It will give you total flexibility to adjust and respond to any response you can possibly hear.

**Unbeliever's likely response**

In general most of the responses that you will hear from the discovery question about the unbeliever's death are uncomplicated. Their answers can be loosely placed into two categories:

- Self glorifying personal works type answers. I've tried to live a good life or be a good person. I have tried to help others and improve myself.

51

- A combination of what they think they believe or do not believe. I believe I will go to heaven because I have lived a good life. I don't believe in hell. I don't believe the Bible has all the answers. Occasionally an unbeliever will identify himself as an atheist. Sometimes they say that because they don't know what they actually believe and do not know what to say. Do not let any response from an unbeliever bother you.

After you hear their response, the goal is to transition to part two of the model and begin to present the Word of God. No matter how unusual their answer may sound, it is the answer that they gave. By responding to them with "That's a normal response," you are acknowledging their right to say whatever they just said and they will appreciate your saying that to them. You are certainly not agreeing with what they said, but are affirming their right to say it. No matter what their response is to the eternal danger question, repeat it back to them in the context of stating that it is a *normal response*.

For example, if they say, *I don't believe in Jesus*, say, "That's a normal response; many people don't believe in Jesus, but let me share something that the Bible says about that for you today." Always be willing to be flexible with whatever their answer or response they give you. The transition/bridge statement will always work for you. It will give you the ability to move to the next part of the soulwinning plan, the presentation of the salvation gospel of Jesus Christ.

It is important to remember that it does not matter how they answer the discovery question. You do not have to address their beliefs or confront them in any way. It was a discovery question for you and for them. For the unbeliever, it allows them to hear and understand what they don't really know and understand. For you, it will instantly locate and identify where the unbeliever is in his understanding of spiritual realities.

The transition statement is a tactic to avoid creating a fight or argument over a "wrong" answer. Or to get over excited because you caught them in a wrong answer and start to challenge what they do not know. By using a strategic transitional statement that shows you respect their answer, they are prepared to be led to the next part of the soulwinning process, which is the introduction of the three scriptures.

The responses of unsaved people will vary, but you can always easily deflect and handle them using this simple transitional technique. It is a sensitive and gentle way for you to maintain control of your presentation and prepare them to become receptive to hear you present the Word of God. This is not the time to confront their answer directly by challenging with something like, *I can't believe you said that!* or *Why would you think that, how can you not believe in God, are you nuts?* It is never a good idea to confront with negative and direct assaults. This is the time to deal with their answer by affirming that whatever they said was normal and using that to lead into your presenting the scriptures.

Remember, don't be alarmed if they say *I don't believe in Jesus, heaven, hell or God.* They are not expected to, they are lost and unsaved. This is a soulwinning process. Let the process work. The overall plan and strategy equips believers to lead unbelievers through a mind field of normal witnessing challenges. The ultimate goal is to gently lead receptive unbelievers to and through the salvation gospel of Jesus Christ and to their salvation. By using this transition/bridge tactic, unbelievers do not feel confronted, condemned or put down and they will remain calm—and so can you. Proverbs 15:1–2 says:

> A soft answer turns away wrath, but a harsh word stirs up anger. The tongue of the wise uses knowledge rightly, but the mouth of fools pours forth foolishness.

Until this point, the goal was to lead the unsaved to respond honestly to what they really don't understand about eternity. The idea behind the transition statement is that after their incorrect or unclear response is established, you can then gently ease them into hearing and receiving the gospel presentation. They may have blurted out that they do not believe in Jesus, heaven, hell, or the Bible. Letting them know this is a normal response for many people allows you to keep moving forward to the ultimate goal of leading them to Christ. This is not the time to argue. After they give their answer, they may want to know what you think about what they just said or what your reaction to it.

Instead of becoming distracted by their response, you lead them into the next functioning part of the model.

## FUNCTION OF PART #2

*"Let me share something with you that the Bible says about that for you today."* This is a very powerful and exciting statement! You are telling an unsaved person that there is something very specific for them from the Bible. The power of that statement is that it will cause them to want to hear what the Bible says for them. Inwardly they are excited, relieved and receptive, because there is an answer for them. They are ready to listen and be taught. They have become receptive and teachable. Through the initial statements and questions about death and telling them that there is something for them from the Bible, you now have them where you want them. You have led them to danger and you are now telling them that there is a Bible answer for them. This is how unbelievers are won to Jesus Christ, by being led to a teachable moment as opposed to a believer trying to verbally tap dance and hope he says something that sticks. The strategy and plan is to bring unbelievers to a mindset wanting to hear God's Word and hear it from you. Unbelievers want to hear the truth and the answer in scripture that you are about to give to them. Unbelievers are now teachable, receptive and ready to hear the Word of God and be won to Jesus Christ as Savior.

### The Word of God is powerful.

The Word of God is power, has power and communicates His power in a way believers can only understand by faith. The four following scriptures underscore the fact that effective witnessing and soulwinning must be rooted in the presentation of the Word of God. It is critical that believers believe and understand the saving power in the clear presentation of the Word of God. The role of believers is to effectively present Jesus Christ and the claims of the cross; it is the business of the Holy Spirit to bring faith to the unbeliever's heart through what he or she hears.

The entire function of part one of this soulwinning plan is to create a teachable moment so that a believer can effectively and successfully present the Word of God. Believers can rely on the Word of God simply because the Word of God says so:

> So shall my word be that goes forth from My mouth. It shall not return to Me void, but it shall accomplish what I please, and it shall prosper in the thing for which I sent it.
>
> —ISAIAH 55:11

> For the Word of God is quick and powerful, and sharper than any two-edged sword, piercing even to the division of soul and spirit, and of joints and marrow, and is a discerner of the thoughts and intents of the heart.
>
> —HEBREWS 4:12

> So then faith comes by hearing and hearing by the Word of God.
>
> —ROMANS 10:17

> All Scripture is given by inspiration of God, and is profitable for doctrine, for reproof, for correction, for instruction in righteousness, that the man of God may be complete, thoroughly equipped for every good work.
>
> —2 TIMOTHY 3:16

These great scriptures establish that in communicating the realities of eternal issues to an unbeliever nothing is as powerful as the Word of God. He separates His words from ours by letting us know that just by hearing His word, something powerful and glorious

55

takes place in the one who hears it. The unsaved can forget or brush aside your words and mine, but the Word of God has power beyond anything that believers can imagine. Always trust the Word of God, stand on it, rely upon it, and above all believe it!

Believers must completely trust and rely on the power in the Word of God in winning souls. The role of the believer is to prepare unbelievers to be teachable and to receive the Word of God. God's Word will answer all the questions an unbeliever has to make their decision for Christ. Believers need no more than a teachable unbeliever and to then present the Word of God, the salvation gospel of Jesus Christ. By presenting and explaining His Word to receptive unbelievers, they can see themselves in the context of what the Bible says for them personally.

Unbelievers will realize they are not some isolated sinner, but are included in all of humanity that needs salvation in Jesus Christ. They are hearing the Word of God receptively because they have been prepared to do so through the eternal danger questions. They want to know answers under these conditions and will listen, receive and respond by receiving Jesus as Savior.

I am communicating this soulwinning plan with words that you can understand. God communicates with words that even unbelievers can understand. Making good decisions is based on good information. The best information is the Word of God. His Word transforms unbelievers, helping them to make good decisions based upon His Word. The power in the Word of God brings unbelievers to an immediate decision to receive Jesus Christ as Savior.

### Three short scriptures

The transition statement leads you to immediately introducing the unbeliever to three short scriptures along with an easily understood, brief explanation of each. These are three of the shortest scriptures in the Bible and are quick and easy to memorize. After you present these verses, you are ready to easily lead the unbeliever through their decision to receive Jesus as Savior. Study and learn the following three scriptures and their significance to the soulwinning model and then, if you haven't already, plan to commit them to memory.

> For all have sinned and come short of the glory of God.
> —ROMANS 3:23

The significance of this scripture is that it shows the broad history of humanity and its disobedience to God. It explains the sin position of an unbeliever in their own personal situation in a gentle way that is easily understood. This helps to move an unsaved person from only seeing others as the bad people because of their bad behavior. It will teach them that everyone is in the same situation as a result of what is generally referred to by theologians as "original sin" or "the fall of man." The unbeliever begins to go through a paradigm shift about their view of sin and who is a sinner. Any preconceived notions about who is bad or who is a sinner must be considered in the light of God's Word that declares "all have sinned." He or she must understand that not just *bad criminals or bad people* are in sin.

You are bringing them to a place where they are beginning to understand that they are spiritually dead. They may not show it, but inwardly an unbeliever will be in shock over this fresh revelation. You are presenting the Word of God and powerfully functioning as God's representative here and now. You are evangelizing an unbeliever, preparing him or her to hear the next scripture in the soulwinning plan.

> For the wages of sin is death, but the gift of God is eternal life through Jesus Christ our Lord.
> —ROMANS 6:23

This verse is presented by dividing it into two sections because in this unique text there is a problem and a solution built into it. The first section presents the *problem:* "For the wages of sin is death." Everyone understands about receiving wages from the work they do. Even unemployed people understand the point.

They have also heard more about death from this verse. The wages of sin are then related to original sin and spiritual death that was just clearly explained to them.

You can now make a very powerful statement to the unsaved person with a simple gesture of pointing towards their heart (I always do): *People who are living and don't know God, in their hearts, know that they don't really know God.* In a tactful and subtle way you are telling them that it is they who do not know God. By the framing of the statement, the unbeliever knows that it is about him or her. You know it's about them, they know it's about them and they know that you know it's about them. The simple gesture just helps with the unspoken confirmation.

Now comes the bad news and the explanation of the ultimate problem. *When that person dies, because he or she didn't know God in this life, he or she won't know God in eternal life. This is when the issue of heaven and hell comes up.* The unsaved person knows that the reference to the person that dies is about him or her. You have been raising the issue of their death. The unsaved know that they do not know God. They are now hearing about a scary reality. People know about heaven and hell. This plan presents a simple reality of hell in a way that the unsaved can catch or grasp their own life and death situation. Believers never need to beat the unbelievers over the head with hell. Unbelievers know exactly what you are talking about and they always get it!

The unsaved are getting a very fast and clear *biblical* education. They are hearing and realizing that the potential to go to hell is not just for imagined bad people from a preconceived notion they may have had. They are beginning to understand that hell is a place for people spiritually separated from God, first in life and then in eternity. You have quickly led an unbeliever to a place where they realize that they are in danger of hell. This is exactly where you want them to be, very fearful about their death and eternal future. They are becoming more deeply evangelized and available for Jesus.

The second section of Romans 6:23 is the *solution*: "... but the gift of God is eternal life through Jesus Christ our Lord." Virtually all unbelievers that believers come in contact with are familiar with the story of Jesus going to the cross. They do not understand the full truth of why He went to the cross, but they know that He did go to the cross. Many will have Jesus in their minds as a good teacher, good person, good example, good religious person of history, or some variation of these examples. Some will view Him as an ascended master along the line of some Eastern religions. Most are familiar with His title as Savior, but do not have a grasp of what His title as Savior ultimately means, particularly to themselves.

In the second part of Romans 6:23, you focus like a laser beam on what Jesus Christ came to do on the cross and why. You clearly explain what all humanity needs to do in response to His glorious work on the cross. The unsaved person will clearly hear that Jesus died for their sins, that their sins are forgiven if they will accept Him and that His sacrifice on the cross was for them personally. The unsaved person knows exactly what you are talking about at this point. In this second part of the text believers are hearing three extremely significant life and death issues. They are hearing them one after another; they are powerful and will not be resisted. These critical issues are:

- Jesus died for their sins.

- Their sins can be forgiven if they accept what Jesus did for them.

- Like others who accept Christ, they will die someday, avoid hell, and have eternity in heaven.

The unsaved person has been confronted in a sensitive and tactful way about death and their option of choosing heaven or hell. At this moment what they are hearing is the fact that they can miss hell and that is very good news for an unsaved person. This far along in the gospel presentation unbelievers are mentally choosing heaven. At the end of this portion of the explanation, the unsaved person has been told what to do to receive eternal life.

**This is a key point.** They are not being asked to respond at this moment. They may want to respond, but this is not the time to ask them to respond, so do not ask them to respond at this point. This is a time to let their desire to respond to Jesus build and build. They are now very deeply evangelized. Their desire and sense of need to come to Christ is building more and more as you continue through to the near conclusion of the salvation gospel presentation.

They have heard why they need to get to heaven and what to do to get to heaven, but have not been asked to do anything to get to heaven. At this moment, this simple tactic of not asking them to do anything is strategic and will increase their receptivity to receive Jesus as Savior. At the conclusion of presenting and explaining Romans 6:23, keep going directly to the third scripture:

> ...that if you confess with your mouth the Lord Jesus and believe in your heart that God has raised Him from the dead, you will be saved.
>
> —ROMANS 10:9

This verse will lead you to the quick and easy conclusion. The unsaved person will be completely with you, they will follow you and will patiently wait for your conclusion. Figuratively, you have them on the edge of their seats! You initially led them to a place of great danger and they know you are about to guide them to a place of great safety. At this point unbelievers want to know how to and want to get to, that place of great safety.

## BRINGING THE UNBELIEVER TO CLOSURE AND SALVATION

The unbeliever has just heard some clearly explained, short and powerful verses that they will know are for them. They have begun to really recognize, understand and realize their sin condition and problem. Unbelievers are clearly hearing, for perhaps the first time, how they, just like all of humanity, need salvation.

Unbelievers realize you are not trying to accuse them of being bad people, but realize that you are educating them to the reality that they, like all of humanity, are fallen from relationship to God through sin. They are ready and will expect you to conclude and help them. Unbelievers may not know exactly how you are going to conclude, but they are ready for it. They are now completely evangelized and prepared to receive the scripture that is at the heart of the salvation gospel of Jesus Christ. Romans 10:9 tells them exactly what to do to receive their salvation in Jesus Christ.

Through this verse you lead the unsaved person directly to a major hot button—hell! As soon as the verse is quoted, you immediately explain what being saved means in a way that is easily understood: *To be saved means a person must be saved from something! They are saved from going to hell and living a life separated from God.* This is a strong and wonderful pronouncement for an unbeliever to hear! These are two powerful and highly motivating things to be saved from. You have the answer for how the unsaved person can be saved from these things and they know it.[1]

The conclusion is to easily bring the unbeliever to salvation. You previously quoted and explained Romans 3:23:

> For all have sinned and come short of the glory of God.

This gave the understanding of why there is a sin problem for all of humanity. In quoting Romans 6:23, you gave them the spiritual problem and solution to the sin condition.

> For the wages of sin is death, but the gift of God is eternal life through Jesus Christ our Lord.

Then you clearly explained that Jesus Christ took their sin upon Himself on the cross, and if they accept Him as Savior, their sins are forgiven and they can have eternal life.

**This is important.** Unbelievers are at this moment digesting what you have just told them and are deeply into their decision-making process. They are making their decision for Jesus Christ and want to be saved!

### A simple question of closure

Immediately ask this question after you quoted and explained Romans 10:9: *"Let me ask you this Joe, would you like to know that you can have eternal life in heaven someday?"*

Wait for their *Yes* response; it will come. Very few, if any, will tell you *No* at this point, after all that they just heard. Most people immediately say, *Yes!* Some almost shout out a very excited, *Yes!* Any resistance to the Word of God has already been broken. This is the moment of decision. The full impact of the Word of God as implemented with the powerful components of the *Witnessing Winzone* plan have moved upon the unsaved person and their incorrect belief systems have imploded and collapsed. The unsaved person has heard as clear a presentation of the salvation gospel as they will ever hear. They heard in a receptive way and will receive it.

Any preconceived notions that the unsaved person had about wrong or false religious concepts are collapsing at this point. Resistance to and misunderstanding of God, Jesus Christ, salvation, eternal life, heaven and hell will disappear because you have led them through this simple and clear roadmap of the Word of God. At this time they will say *yes* because they have already surrendered.

As soon as they say *yes* or indicate a *yes* with a nod—most often they will answer with a solid *Yes!* —make the following clear statement to close out the witness. At this point they are ready to pray and this explanation is simply giving some direction about how this process will conclude. They will completely follow your directions:

*Okay, I'd like to lead you in a short prayer. This will be your prayer. We are going to invite Jesus Christ to be your Savior, forgive you of your sins and give you eternal life. I will lead the prayer; you just repeat the prayer. Will you pray with me?* (Wait for yes; it will come.)

*Joe, this is your prayer. I will lead you in the prayer; you just repeat the prayer.* (They may go blank for a moment; they have heard a lot and you may have to restate slowly.... ....*Joe, this is your prayer; I will lead you in the prayer; you just repeat the prayer.*) (Take their hand if appropriate; I almost always do.) *Heavenly Father, I accept Jesus Christ as my Savior. I ask you to forgive me of my sins and give me eternal life, and I will seek your will for my life. In Jesus name I pray. Amen.*

The invitation to pray sequence is a clear and uncomplicated direction for an unbeliever to pray to receive Jesus as Savior. To further encourage an unbeliever to pray, you include yourself by saying, *we are going to invite Jesus Christ to be your Savior*.... .... The only thing that you asked of them here is simply, *Will you pray with me?* This low key offer to pray with them was set up and prepared through the presentation and strategy in the soulwin-ning plan. It is a low key, non threatening offer to pray and easy for unbelievers to respond to. In bringing the *Witnessing Winzone* presentation to closure, ultimately the only thing that the unsaved person is asked to do is to pray to receive Christ with you. They were asked several questions, but the only thing that they were asked to do was to pray with you.

Do not be alarmed or nervous if you feel you do not know an appropriate sinner's prayer. There is no perfected or secret sinner's prayer locked in a safe somewhere that only a select few can see and use. Use the model sinner's prayer that was just presented, expand it, or feel free to develop a simple one of your own.

## HOW TO HANDLE AN UNBELIEVER'S QUESTIONS

An unbeliever may suddenly interrupt and ask you a question in the middle of your presentation. It will probably be about some-thing that you can easily answer. If you can give an extremely brief answer or explanation, do so. However, usually the best way to answer is as follows: *That is a good question, I will get to it as soon as I am through with this scripture.*

The goal is for you to win the unsaved person to Christ, not for you to be a Bible- answers-person. Do not think that you have to answer a laundry list of their questions. Answer their questions, of course, but on your terms, not theirs. Under no circumstances let an unbeliever take you off track. You keep them on track. You are in charge of this critical witness process, not the unsaved person.

You are leading and controlling the witnessing and soulwinning process by asking strategic questions. Unbelievers can try and wrest control of the process by asking their own strategic questions. Usually their strategy is to take the process in the direction that they want it to go in. Unbelievers are used to being in control and may try to take it back through asking questions. This is spiritual warfare. Don't let them, by assuming that their questions are merely innocent curiosity. You ask questions for several reasons and they do as well. Maintain your direction and control by deflecting their questions until you want to deal with them, not when they want to deal with them.

While you have learned the complete soulwinning model from these chapters, you will want to do more than to simply memorize the steps and the scriptures and questions involved. In order to become effectively equipped to win unbelievers to Christ using the *Witnessing Winzone* plan, you will need to make a commitment to learn and thoroughly understand this approach to soulwinning.

# 4

# Do More Than Memorize the Plan

FOR ANY BELIEVER TO BE effective in soulwinning, he or she must make a commitment to completely learn the *Witnessing Winzone* soulwinning plan. This is going to be more than just a soulwinning model for memorization. This is a challenge to do more than just simply memorize the basic questions and scriptures; it means taking ownership of it by understanding it to the core of your soul. It means for believers to memorize and know it so well that there is a smooth flow of unbroken presentation of the gospel.

Most of us can recall in our elementary school years being called on to memorize and recite a poem at school. Some of those early attempts probably had hesitation and embarrassing pauses associated with the effort. Believers need to make an effort that goes beyond just a basic memory exercise. It needs to be an uncompromised commitment of memorization to a point of knowing and understanding your soulwinning plan so well that you have an ability to present your soulwinning plan without hesitation or stumbling. No hesitation means no stumbling through the process. No hesitation means no... *Well, uh...let me see, ah...!* I encourage you to apply a high level of maturity, professionalism and care when learning this soulwinning plan. Souls are at stake. It is not hard to learn, and the believers who make the effort to learn it will become successful beyond anything imaginable.

## PREPARED
## vs. UNPREPARED WITNESSING

To be prepared or not be prepared is a critical question in witnessing and soulwinning. Actually, being prepared or not determines whether or not you will consistently see soulwinning results. There are believers who will argue about style vs. substance. Style in witnessing represents the methodology believers rely on in their approach to personal evangelism. Style has to do with a believer's point of view in how a witnessing exchange unfolds, for example, whether planned or unplanned. The *Witnessing Winzone* strategic biblical soulwinning plan represents a planned or prepared style.

If someone says, *I don't need to learn or memorize anything; I just trust the Lord and believe Him for results*, that particular witnessing style would be a simple example of a well-intentioned, unprepared style of witnessing. That attitude may work for an experienced, gifted evangelist, but for most believers it will lead to zero results and witnessing burn-out. As well–meaning as that statement might be, it is an approach to witnessing that I believe should and can easily be upgraded to the *Witnessing Winzone* soulwinning plan.

Any particular style means little if it does not result in the salvation of souls. The result of a witnessing exchange can be a decision or a non-decision for Christ. Let me pose a question. Is there more validation in a salvation when an unprepared believer wins an unbeliever, than when a prepared believer wins an unbeliever? Of course not! The witnessing focus is on the result, which should be winning a soul to Christ.

Just as preparation is a key to success in any endeavor, it is a vital part of witnessing and winning souls. Some believers may feel a reluctance regarding planned soulwinning presentations. That kind of reaction may stem from a false perception that a planned soulwinning approach means trying to *program* witnessing. A realistic view of witnessing is that no believer can be completely programmed to witness and witness effectively.

A witness exchange has a life of its own, with its own ebb and flow. Some believers may feel hesitant about having a prepared presentation because they feel it would not be natural. What feels natural now is what believers are doing now. There may be no substance in what they are doing, but since this is what is being done now, this is what feels natural now. What is important is the result; is it winning souls?

The fact is that as soon as someone learns it, the soulwinning plan feels natural. Feeling natural is a relative term. A person's preference can be to be prepared or unprepared. Either one can feel natural. The power of being completely prepared with the plan is seen in the following:

- You already know the direction of the witnessing exchange and what you are going to say.

- You are prepared with a response for whatever an unsaved person will say.

- You will experience great assurance with freedom from fear and intimidation.

- In almost all witness exchanges, you already know the outcome—a lost soul won to Christ!

## PASTORS, ACTORS, AND SALESPEOPLE

If I have a conversation with anyone who has not experienced the freedom, assurance and creativity that comes from having a planned soulwinning presentation, I always try to explain my approach by referring to three groups of effective communicators who use prepared presentations:

- First, pastors always plan their sermons. They are well thought out, studied, and to some extent, rehearsed. Pastors want their message to have an opening, several main points and a solid closing. They want to lead the congregation to the conclusion that they believe God has for them through the message. Pastors take courses in homiletics when they are students in Bible colleges and seminaries for the purpose of learning how to plan their sermons. In preaching classes there is instruction of how to stand, how to make proper emphasis through gestures from the pulpit, etc. When pastors or evangelists speak from pulpits they are prepared through their experience and with planned presentations called sermons. This preparation gives them the assurance to minister freely and allow the Holy Spirit to minister through them a message that is effective for the people.

- Second, every time an actor in Hollywood wins an Academy Award it is from memorizing a prepared presentation. In Hollywood they call it a script. They learn their lines word-for-word and then blend them with their personality and role. They do not let the words control them, they control the words through their personalities in their character development. Actors know what they are supposed to say and this gives them the freedom to be themselves and adapt, adjust, and be creative in their presentation.

- Third, a sales person is successful because of good work habits and planned sales presentations that lead to deal-closing results. Sales people are consistently successful because they always know what they are doing with their presentations. To be successful in sales there is little guess work. Successful sales people know how potential customers will react to what they tell or ask them. They generally assume leadership in the dialogue with their potential customers and these customers are never aware they are being led or directed. Like actors with scripts, salespeople with sales presentations do not let words control them. They learn their presentations and let their own personality come through as they present their products, goods or services.

I am not equating selling products, goods and services with presenting Jesus Christ. In am only pointing out that there are similarities of process between winning souls and selling. For example, in soulwinning and making sales there is always communication, a presentation and then a moment of decision and closure. The common denominator that pastors, actors, and salespeople share with you is that they learn, commit to memory, and are prepared when they communicate. After they have learned what is needed, they are then free to be themselves.

## PREPARATION IS FREEDOM

It is this preparation that eliminates the fear, intimidation and confusion factor in witnessing. By being prepared and getting the preparation part out of the way, the fear, intimidation and confusion factor will get out of the way. A planned soulwinning presentation will not restrict a believer; quite the opposite, it will free a believer to communicate ideas easily about eternal matters. It will free a believer to be themselves. Because there is a planned direction, the fear of the unknown is eliminated. When the fear of the unknown is eliminated, intimidation is eliminated. With no plan and direction in witnessing there is generally confusion about what to do or say next. When believers are unprepared they are and remain trapped in a box of doubt, fear and insecurity of what is taking place in witnessing encounters. When believers are prepared they can come out of the box of doubt, fear and insecurity. Prepared and equipped believers have a real sense of becoming free to be used of God powerfully in witnessing and winning souls. Jesus said, "And you shall know the truth, and the truth shall make you free"(Jn. 8:32).

I am certainly not advocating that you have to become a pastor, actor, or salesperson to effectively win souls. These are just three examples of people who get prepared with planned preparations in order to be effective. They also live lives that require a constant change and upgrade of their respective presentations. Fortunately for you, with this soulwinning plan you only have to learn it once and you are set for life!

Words can be stiff sounding or stiff feeling, but people do not have to be. Believers should always know what they are talking about and doing, with a sense of freedom, when witnessing to a nonbeliever. Once equipped and prepared you will be thrilled at how flexible and creative you can be in effectively presenting the gospel of Jesus Christ. Preparation will give you freedom and will release you out of any box of limitation as a result of being unprepared.

The *Witnessing Winzone* is a planned presentation of the gospel that gives you precise direction when you want to bring closure to general witnessing and win the unsaved person to Christ. If you will totally incorporate this plan into your witnessing and adapt it to your personality, you can become as successful in personal evangelism as you want to be.

> By failing to prepare . . . You are preparing to fail.
> —BENJAMIN FRANKLIN

## MOST BELIEVERS
## WANT NURTURING RELATIONSHIPS

It almost goes without saying that most believers are willing to have relationships with unbelievers. The concept of relational evangelism always takes place by the virture of believers knowing and interacting with unbelievers. A believer may or may not have a deep relationship with an unbeliever. Relationships with unbelievers develop at many relational levels. It is important to keep pursuing relationship with unbelievers. Relationships can be old, new, casual, or temporary. A challenge believers face in developing relationships with unbelievers is that not all unbelievers want a deep relationship with them.

Initiating or attempting to initiate relationship with unbelievers is biblical and healthy. Relationships with unbelievers can be unpredictable and the depth of the relationship is also going to be unpredictable. Believers may think they have one relationship with an unbeliever and the reality is the relationship is different than they thought. Winning an unbeliever to Jesus Christ does not depend upon the depth of the relationship. Relationships offer evangelistic opportunities but believers must still know how to handle any level of relationship from an evangelistic perspective. That perspective is always sensitive to the opportunity to win the unbeliever to Jesus Christ.

> For though I am free from all men, I have made myself a servant to all, that I might win the more; and to the Jews I became as a Jew, that I might win Jews; to those who are under the law, as under the law, that I might win those who are under the law; to those who are without law, as without law (not being without law toward God, but under the law toward Christ), that I might win those who are without law; to the weak I became as weak, that I might win the weak, I have become all things to all men, that I might by all means save some.
>
> 1 CORINTHIANS 9:19–22

## KEEP THE PROCESS MOVING

Ongoing friendly communication is nurturing because it keeps a door open for sustained witnessing. The Holy Spirit will create the right time to win an unbeliever. Constant analysis and depth of a relationship as the standard to win a soul can be a major challenge for most believers. How many close relationships do believers have or does anyone have? Particularly close relationships between believers and unbelievers are rare. At times these close relationships exist because the believer never brings up the need to come to Christ. The unbeliever may have already established the conditions and control of an ongoing relationship. They do that with pronouncements like, "Being a Christian is good for you. You live your life, I'll live mine, and we'll be friends."

Relationships are subjective processes. Every believer must make their own decisions about how to handle them with unbelievers. A heavy weight is placed upon believers when they are told the only way to win souls is through their capacity to develop deep relationships. The extreme mindset in relational evangelism is something like, "If there is no deep relationship, then all other personal evangelism is invalid." Deep relationships are good when they develop but do not have to be the criteria to win souls. Most of the time all that is necessary to win a soul is when a believer has an open line of friendly communication with an unbeliever. It could be an ongoing relationship or an instantaneous new one. A healthy balance is to be equipped to win any believer to Christ no matter what the level of relationship. Most of the time the deeper the relationship with an unbeliever won to Christ the better, for follow-up and discipleship encouragement. These new believers like everyone else always have many variables in their lifestyle. They move, change jobs, don't like a particular church, an so on. Believers should be equipped to win them, direct and encourage them, but most of all trust them to the Holy Spirit—to trust the Holy Spirit to lead these new believers to the future He has for them.

## ASSURANCE TO SPEAK
## TO AN OCCASIONAL STRANGER

Earlier I mentioned that after you have learned this approach to witnessing you would lead people to Christ in the most interesting places. Many times I have pulled up to a convenience store or a service station with no thought about witnessing. Someone would be outside either standing around or leaving and the Lord would prompt me that I was to lead that person to Christ. Don't let that kind of situation make you nervous, because winning a stranger to Christ is the easiest of all. It is the easiest because you are anonymous. They don't know you and you don't know them. There is nothing to lose and everything to gain. False fears are built up in believers as a result of not knowing what they would say to a complete stranger.

When talking to a stranger all that has to be said is, hello, my name is _____. I am a Christian; I do evangelism work and I talk to a lot of people about Jesus Christ, salvation and eternal life. May I ask you a question without being too personal? We are all going to die someday, right? What I would like to ask you is this, When you die and its time for you to go to heaven and Jesus Christ asks you............ Then just continue!

You may ask, Are you kidding? Is it that simple? The answer is YES! It is that simple. Keep in mind you are catching people off guard and they are unprepared and not on the defensive. You are the one prepared and on the offensive to win them. You may ask why I use the term *evangelism work?* You say that because that is what you are doing at that moment and the statement adds immediate credibility to you personally. You are not claiming to be an evangelist, but you are doing evangelism work.

On an airplane you may introduce yourself to your seat partner, have some small talk and possibly share that you are a Christian or go to church. Begin to lightly witness. If you sense it is the appropriate time, just simply say to the unsaved person, calling them by their first name, "_____, I talk to a lot of people about Jesus Christ, salvation and eternal life. May I ask you a question without being too personal?" Then continue!

## SPEAKING OF AIRPLANES

I was once on an airplane and before take-off there was a long wait. I was in the window seat and a rather upset lady was in the aisle seat. We were talking and very quickly the conversation turned to spiritual needs and concerns. It was a good and engaging conversation when suddenly a man sat down in the seat between us and started reading his newspaper. She looked at me and I looked at her and we both knew we wanted to keep talking. We both leaned forward and talked around and behind the other passenger's newspaper. It was in this unusual position that I introduced the soulwinning plan and led her to salvation. The man in the middle never moved, but I know he heard every word. This woman was so interested in her salvation that she actually leaned around a man reading a newspaper to get saved!

## FLEXIBLE FOR ANY SITUATION

No matter what sort of scenario you can think of, you can use the *Witnessing Winzone* plan to fit it or adjust to it. When you learn the soulwinning plan so well that you can recite it in your sleep, you will realize the flexibility that is built into it. Learn it, use it and you will experience immediate success, which will encourage you to keep going forward in winning souls. Unbelievers are everywhere and you will encounter soulwinning opportunities everywhere. You, as an equipped–to–win souls believer, will be shocked at the many opportunities the Lord will provide for you to win souls. These opportunities will come in your family, friends, work associates and yes, even an occasional stranger.

When Jesus revealed Himself to the Samaritan woman at the well (See John 4:1–26), she was a stranger to Him. When Phillip led the Ethiopian eunuch to Jesus as Savior, the eunuch was a stranger to him. Keep in mind that a stranger is merely a person you have not yet met. Have you ever asked someone you did not know for directions or information about something. Winning a person you do not know is just as easy. Be prepared when the Lord prompts you to witness and win perhaps, an occasional stranger.

You may be shocked at how easy it is to win someone you do not know the first time you do it. When Jesus was explaining to Nicodemus that being born again is of the Spirit, He declared: "The wind blows where it wishes, and you hear the sound of it, but cannot tell where it comes from and where it goes. So is everyone who is born of the spirit" (Jn. 3:8). The Holy Spirit will direct believers to unbelievers in situations that He has orchestrated and when He does you will be prepared. Whenever I feel led to speak to a stranger to win them, I almost never introduce myself as a pastor. I believe that to suddenly announce to an unbeliever that a pastor is talking to them may shock or even turn them off. I simply introduce myself as a Christian doing evangelism work, as I have explained.

## IT'S NOT WHAT YOU SAY, BUT HOW YOU SAY IT

According to one study, there are more elements involved in true communication than our words, or what we say. In fact, words have the smallest influence of all the elements of communication. According to the study, of what we communicate to others, only 7 percent has to do with words; 55 percent has to do with body language, and 35 percent has to do with tone of voice. Even the environment is responsible for 3 percent of the influence of our communications. So it is important to pay attention to how we communicate to others.

To help an unsaved person to be at ease, you need to be at ease in posture and demeanor. Speak softly with the powerful words of God. Let your entire demeanor reflect tenderness and sensitivity to the unsaved person you want to win. It is amazing that around 90 percent of the communication process on a personal level has to do with the smile on your face, the warm gaze of your eye, the posture of your body and the gentleness in your voice. The words that are spoken make up a small portion of communication. Words convey knowledge; facial expression, intent of the eye, and body posture convey caring. People read you more than they listen to you.

Believers should be sensitive as they strategically present the powerful words of God, and if they are, they will be successful. Communication has been described as an art form. This soulwinning plan will give you a way to exercise the art form of communication in personal evangelism as never before. The percentages presented for the communication equation are based on everyday words used in communication. When believers communicate the Word of God, communication is raised to another level in the communication dynamic. That is why is so important to rely on God's Word when we witness.

God communicates with words that we understand, His written word, Holy Scripture. Believers present God's written word that even unbelievers can understand. Your words and mine are not powerful, but the Word of God is powerful. It is so powerful it communicates with an unsaved soul. How long do you think it takes to make a decision? On some matters people may think, ponder and do extensive research, and spend hours, days, weeks or years. But when it comes to making the actual decision, they make it in a millisecond. Getting the right information is one thing, but making the decision when a person has the right information is immediate.

> For the Word of God is quick, and powerful, and sharper than any two edged sword, piercing even to the dividing asunder of soul and spirit, and of the joints and marrow, and is a discerner of the thoughts and intents of the heart.
> —HEBREWS 4:12, KJV

## EXPOSE THE TRUTH OF WHAT THEY DON'T KNOW

The strategy of the *Witnessing Winzone* prepares unbelievers to face their own uncertainties about eternal life. They have been led into the strategic statement and question sequence specifically to help them become educated and unsure about what they think or believe about Jesus and eternity. In most witnessing exchanges the unsaved are in control because they know believers want something from them, and they dodge and weave and will reveal little. At the end of some of these witness encounters unsaved people just walk away and believers don't know why they didn't come to Christ. Through this plan, as I explained it, that situation is reversed. Through the eternal danger question you get an unbeliever to voice an unsure statement that they ordinarily would not do. It is an exposed statement regarding what they think or believe about their own death.

When unbelievers voice an unsure statement, they are fully aware of their uncertainty and immediately become more receptive about hearing more. Unbelievers almost never want you to know that they are unsure. What has been accomplished is they have been led into revealing and exposing their lack of true knowledge about the issues surrounding their own death. By stating an unclear or unsure answer, unbelievers will realize what they really do not understand and they will be completely receptive to your leadership. They realize they have exposed their unsure knowledge issues and know that you know it as well. The unsaved will be quite vulnerable and how you handle their position of vulnerability is vital at this moment.

## UNBELIEVERS THINK THEIR GOOD WORKS GET THEM TO HEAVEN

Most of the time unbelievers will answer with something like, *I've tried to be a good person* or *I've tried to live a good life*. They have been asked an unexpected question and will not know how to handle it. Their basic reaction will be an answer out of their good works rationalization. That is why you will hear over and over a variation of *I've tried to be a good person* or things like, *because my uncle was a church deacon*. Be prepared to hear all kinds of unusual responses. Do not allow yourself to become amused at unusual answers. Maintain a calm demeanor.

Some will actually say they *deserve* to go to Heaven. Many times the answer of an unsaved person will have a self-righteous quality. It is the *good works* mentality. Most unsaved people see themselves as good and assume that since they see themselves as good, all that they do or have done is generally in a good category. They may feel that occasionally they make mistakes or use bad judgment, but unbelievers always believe that they are good. That is the self-image that most unsaved persons want for themselves and they want you to believe that image as well. The unsaved will almost always give a self-glorifying response whether they actually believe it or not. Occasionally some will honestly reply, *I don't know.* It is interesting to note Jesus' perspective regarding the "good" category:

> Now a certain ruler asked Him, saying, "Good Teacher, what shall I do to inherit eternal life?" So Jesus said to him, "Why do you call Me good? No one is good but One, that is, God."
> —LUKE 18:18–19

## THE UNSAVED HAVE REASONS TO RESIST

Several reasons exist for the evasiveness of unsaved people in witness exchanges. Being aware of and understanding the following explanations will help you as you witness:

- Unsaved persons want to protect and keep hidden what they believe and think in order to avoid personal responsibility for their sin condition. They will not even acknowledge their sin condition. They are fully aware of their thought life and behavior. Most unsaved people have difficulty acknowledging wrongdoing, certainly from a sin perspective. They hide and protect who they really are to escape your judgment. They are very sensitive about what a Christian believer will think of them. They may revel in and love their sin lifestyle, but they want it secret and unrevealed. Some of the more common responses that unbelievers hide behind are: I'll think about it, I'll read the Bible about that, I'll talk about it later and That's good for you, but I live my own life. There are countless varieties of these evasive responses. Unbelievers are non-commital and generally do not want a Christian to know what they really don't know or understand.

- As long as an unbeliever can maintain a hidden, evasive and protective face they can maintain control. This is their personal safety wall. They know that the believer is the one doing the fishing. They don't want to get caught. An unbeliever can be quite skilled at being evasive. It is their ability to dodge and weave that gives them control of the witness exchange. For some unbelievers it simply becomes a game, a game of hide and seek.

- Unbelievers do not always know who to trust or believe. They have heard all the talk about cults, false religion, and ministries that have had problems. The unsaved are not in the dark on problem issues surrounding the body of Christ. Adding to the problem, throughout the last half of the twentieth Century and continuing today has been an ongoing assault on the body of Christ through various forms of media.

- Unbelievers are generally apprehensive of spiritual change. This is referring primarily to unsaved adults. Youth are willing to step out by faith, but mature adults are leery of new things that are so significant. Receiving Jesus Christ represents a major life change.

- Unbelievers don't want to feel taken advantage of or exploited. The unsaved have concerns of someone taking advantage of them. They feel vulnerable because they are unsaved. They like a sense of safety. Coming to Christ represents the challenge of coming out of their comfort zone.

- An unbeliever may have had a bad experience in a church as a child. They may have had a bad experience with a Christian person at an earlier time. Past negative witnessing experiences can create a huge defensive attitude towards Christians. There have been situations when well meaning or not so well meaning believers put some unbelievers through a witnessing wringer. Over the years I have had several conversations with unbelievers

who conveyed to me that they felt that some believers
had improperly or even illegally harassed them.

- Many unbelievers have dabbled in a combination of false
  religions, cults, astrology, New Age philosophy and Eastern Mysticism. They are aware or think they know a little
  of one religion or another and may be convinced there
  are many ways to God.

No matter what the religious background or history is of an unbeliever, they will respond to a loving believer who will gently lead
them to Jesus as Savior. The strategy in this soulwinning plan brushes
away the concerns surrounding all of these issues. It does that because
it is grounded in the Word of God and the strategy is the unique
introduction to the presentation of the Word of God.

## WINNING SOULS IS THE FIRST STEP

The primary mission of *Witnessing Winzone* is equipping the body
of Christ to perform the function of winning souls into the kingdom of God. In Matthew 28:19, Jesus' command is clear:

> Go therefore and make disciples of all the nations, baptizing
> them in the name of the Father and of the Son and of the
> Holy Spirit, teaching them to observe all things that I have
> commanded you; and lo, I am with you always, even to the
> end of the age.

In this verse that is called the Great Commission, Jesus is calling
for more than just winning souls. He wants more for new believers than just a salvation that is fire insurance from hell. Salvation
from hell is certainly no small thing. John 3:16 states that He was
sent so the world would not perish: "For God so loved the world
that He gave His only begotten Son, that whoever believes in Him
should not perish but have everlasting life." But He wants believers to go beyond basic eternal safety; He is commanding believers to disciple new believers. Discipling means to nurture, teach,

assist, and guide a new believer away from a self-centered life into a mature, Christ-centered life. The goal is a life that fully reflects a life in Him. Jesus has underscored His focus on making disciples because the heart of our heavenly Father goes beyond just getting people saved from their sins. He wants a total restoration of His human creation that was lost to Him. Salvation must be experienced before discipleship can begin.

An unbeliever can be in a partial discipleship process by virtue of simply being consistently present in a Bible-believing church. Discipleship in the lives of believers on one level or another is a life-long process. Christians must always grow, mature and continually deepen in the things of God. Therefore the heartbeat of the Church is to win souls, disciple and make disciples who will win souls and be a part of discipling others. In the Great Commission text Jesus does not specifically say "Go and win souls." I believe there are several reasons He did not use those words.

- First, He didn't need to say it. Making disciples presupposes that individuals have already been saved, i.e. won to Christ. The church does not disciple unbelievers.

- Second, the focus of the Great Commission text is discipleship. It underscores the fact that He wants believers to be discipled and not just saved.

- Third, He does state it indirectly through His reference to being baptized "in the name of the Father and of the Son and of the Holy Spirit." Jesus is going far beyond John's baptism of repentance. He is declaring new believers must be baptized in the Trinity, which means salvation has taken place in Jesus Christ, the Son.

Occasionally, someone will comment that in the Great Commission it does not say "Go and win souls," but only to make disciples. This kind of observation sometimes has a slightly negative tone, that implies that when anyone exhorts others to win souls they do not value discipleship. Balancing the Great Commission in Matt 28:19 that calls for discipleship with the salvation concerns expressed in John 3:16 is an exciting subject. It is always a glorious event to win an unsaved person to Jesus Christ. Having stated that, the circumstances surrounding every single person won to Christ may not be perfect from a discipleship perspective. The Great Commission tells the church that Jesus Christ's emphasis is on making disciples. That is the mission of the church in the body of Christ.

I believe there is a balance for believers to understand that it is always good to win an unbeliever to Christ no matter where or when—and always to encourage discipleship. As souls are won to Christ, these new believers should be encouraged to get involved in a good Bible–believing church. And when it is possible, you should follow up to help them become established in the body of Christ.

## THE DISCIPLESHIP CHALLENGE

The discipleship process cannot always unfold in ways that fit every believer's particular ideas about how discipleship must take place. Sometimes circumstances prevent personally discipling a new believer. The basic alternatives in discipleship are in a personal follow-up context:

- Invite the new believer to your home church.
- Disciple a new believer on your own.
- Refer a new believer to another person or church.

I believe it is important to encourage believers to not hesitate to win souls because they might think, "*Who would disciple the individual if I can't? So why bother?!* Believers who are winning souls will never see all new believers discipled where believers think they should be. Believers must be willing to trust the leadership of the Holy Spirit in the life of any new believer. The Holy Spirit must be relied upon no matter what or where anyone comes to Christ, in a church or otherwise. Believers must trust and believe that the

Holy Spirit can and will direct new believers. At the very least the Holy Spirit will begin a fresh work in the life of a new believer whether he or she understands it or not. The Holy Spirit will lead them on their next step in Christ that takes them to where they can grow in Him. Believers must trust the Holy Spirit to do His part; He will always do His part. When needed, He will safely lead the new believer to the next person or group of believers where they can be discipled.

It is my experience that when someone declares or implies that it does no good to win an unbeliever to Christ without personally seeing them discipled, that person is frustrated with two evangelism and discipleship issues:

- First they are equating sowing and reaping as one. Sowing is witnessing with no salvation result. Reaping is a decision for Christ, a soul won to Him. The difference between the two is eternal. A believer may hear hesitancy from a new believer to come to church and question whether the person was really saved or not. A new believer may not be responding to overtures the way a believer thinks they should be at a particular time.

- I believe they are also frustrated because of a previous experience of seeing someone they were ministering to leave the church. The person that left is then perceived as having *drifted away* from the Lord. This may have happened when someone left a church under difficult circumstances. It could come from any number of reasons. Somehow a discipleship process ended prematurely and the conclusion was reached that it was a waste of time. The bottom line is a mindset was developed that it does no good to win souls unless it is under a tight discipleship control situation. Believers must always trust the Lord for souls won in sometimes very unusual circumstances. New believers sometimes do things and sometimes there is no apparent reason that is easy to understand. It is then easy to assume the worst.

## WHAT HAPPENS TO THESE NEW BELIEVERS?

Some believers are discipled where they receive salvation and some are not. By accepting Jesus as Savior through the *Witnessing Winzone* the unbeliever has heard and responded to the salvation gospel. At times the new believer must be trusted to the Holy Spirit as he or she goes on their way.

For example, when Philip and the eunuch parted, the scripture says that Philip was caught away, so that the eunuch saw him no more; and he went on his way rejoicing (Acts 8:37–39) In John 3:8, Jesus is explaining to Nicodemus that being born again means being born of the Spirit. He declared: "The wind blows where it wishes, and you hear the sound of it, but cannot tell where it comes from and where it goes. So is everyone who is born of the spirit." That same Spirit will not leave a newly won believer in Jesus Christ as an orphan. He will guide him or her to be established in the body of Christ. As the scripture declares:

> For He Himself has said, "I will never leave you nor forsake you."
>
> —HEBREWS 13:5

### A part of my personal testimony

Over the years I have talked with many believers who were won to Christ in unusual situations and ended up in other locations or churches later, sometimes much later. Part of my own testimony is that many years ago in Beaumont, Texas, I went forward during an invitation for salvation given by a pastor on a beautiful Sunday morning. When I came forward my exact words to the pastor were, "I come to be a Christian." In hindsight, when I said that, what I really meant was, "I want to become a Christian; what do I do?" He must have assumed that I had already accepted Jesus as Savior and I was baptized that night. In his excitement for me, he neglected to lead me through any form of a sinner's prayer to receive Jesus as my personal Savior. I got baptized, but was not born again. He was a great preacher and I never forgot the pastor's preaching about Jesus being a personal Savior.

Five years later, I was struggling to find a new direction in life. I had moved to Hollywood, was working and studying at an actor's studio, but was unfulfilled. Hollywood was fun and a great experience, but I knew I needed something more. On May 2, 1977 in Hollywood, California, I prayed this salvation prayer in my apartment: "Jesus, if you are who people say you are, be my Savior and help me in my life." In that instant, I was gloriously born again and my life began anew. The Lord led me to a little Southern Baptist church called First Baptist Beverly Hills where a body of believers loved me and helped to disciple me.

It was about a week or two after this that I first won someone to Christ. The first person I led to the Lord was a young lady at my apartment swimming pool in Hollywood. I was sharing with her how I had accepted Jesus, but was not sure beyond that how to explain salvation to her. I excused myself, went into my apartment and called a new good friend and brother in the Lord, John Webb, who was the Minister of Music at First Baptist. He directed me to read Romans 10:9 to her, and I clumsily took her through it. She prayed to receive Jesus with me that hour, and John and I later ministered to her. I didn't see her again until eight or nine years later. One night she saw me at a church concert and came up to me to share what had happened to her. She said that at a time later she had become severely ill and was hospitalized, but through that experience she had come into contact with some other believers that ministered to her. She said she never forgot praying with me and knew that the Lord was with her. She was currently ministering with a praise group, and I have not seen her since. It is always quite interesting to hear how the Lord worked in a person's life and it was not how someone else thought it was supposed to happen.

Believers want to know what happens to those that they touch and win to Jesus Christ. Unfortunately, it is just not always possible to know. When a believer is equipped to use the *Witnessing Winzone* plan, he or she will become soulwinners for the rest of their lives. They will do so in countless situations and many unusual scenarios. Successful soulwinning encounters will not always take place under conditions that some may consider to be ideal. It would be ideal for anyone who comes to Christ to become part of a discipling process as quickly as possible. A new believer should become part of a Bible believing church as soon as possible. It is just not always possible after winning someone to Christ to personally influence their discipleship training.

At these times believers must trust these new believers to the same Lord Who has become their Savior. Remember the thief on the cross? God saves people in extreme situations and takes responsibility for their care:

> Then one of the criminals who were hanged blasphemed Him, saying, 'If you are the Christ, save Yourself and us.' But the other, answering, rebuked him, saying, 'Do you not even fear God, seeing your are under the same condemnation? And we indeed justly, for we receive the due reward of our deeds; but this Man has done nothing wrong.' Then he said to Jesus, 'Lord remember me when You come into Your kingdom.' And Jesus said to him, 'Assuredly, I say to you, today you will be with Me in Paradise.'
>
> —Luke 23:39–43

# 5

# Biblical Truth Impacts

EVANGELISM AS MISSION IS THE broad function of the body of Christ. To evangelize as analyzed here, is dealing with an individual or individuals; specifically, how to evangelize an individual unbeliever. When most Christians evangelize, they will evangelize one or two unbelievers at a time. *The Witnessing Winzone* soulwinning plan can be used to evangelize a small group, and it can also be quite effective in large audience invitations. For an unsaved person to be deeply evangelized, they must be greatly impacted with a combination of truths and realities about the gospel of Jesus Christ. To be evangelized means an unsaved person has been impacted and drawn to Jesus Christ by the power of God through implementing several biblical references and components.

It is not enough for them to just hear general scriptures or references about the gospel of Christ, but they must hear the gospel presented in a way that has a multifaceted impact upon them personally. For the unsaved to be powerfully evangelized, they must be powerfully impacted and when done correctly, saving faith in Christ is quickened in them by the Holy Spirit.

The following are ten critical, interactive components that will evangelize, which means impacting, an unbeliever toward their decision to receive Jesus Christ as Savior. Ideally, these components should be present in any witnessing exchange that attempts to evangelize an unsaved person.

By identifying these ten components, I do not mean to suggest or imply that sharing less than these components in witnessing totally prohibits the evangelizing of an unsaved person or that they cannot otherwise be evangelized. However, all of the following components, when working in concert together, will absolutely impact and deeply evangelize an unbeliever. They are what make the *Witnessing Winzone* soulwinning plan such a powerful evangelistic tool:

- You, the believer, ministering the gospel of Jesus Christ through this prepared soulwinning plan. The Word of God you present will greatly impact the life of the unbeliever. You, the witnessing believer, are the point person for all other components to be able to work. Your trust in what His Word can do is vital for the ministering believer as well as for the unbeliever. The key to this plan is that the believer is the one to guide the unsaved person through strategic questions into an attitude of receptivity in order to present the Word of God and then let the Word of God do its mighty work. You have a work to do. The Word of God has a work to do. And the Holy Spirit has a work to do.

- The work of the Holy Spirit. Jesus will draw people to Himself through the power of the Holy Spirit. Remember Jesus' last words on earth just before He ascended: "But you shall receive power when the Holy Spirit has come upon you; and you shall be witnesses to Me in Jerusalem, and in all Judea and Samaria, and to the end of the earth (Acts 1:8). In the midst of any witness exchange, believers will be empowered by the Holy Spirit to carry out Jesus' great call for his or her life.

- A message about the Heavenly Father and His will for humanity. Unbelievers must hear of God as Creator, His

Holiness and His command for humanity to live lives of holiness and righteousness.

- A message about Jesus Christ and His atoning work on the cross. The message is that He is the answer to the eternal questions surrounding death, eternal life and how to get to Heaven. They need to hear that Jesus died for all of humanity, but that individually, people must choose to receive Him as Savior. It is the message of John 3:16: "For God so loved the world that He gave His only begotten Son, that whoever believes in Him should not perish but have everlasting life" It must show that Jesus is the only way to God: "I am the way, the truth, and the life. No one comes to the Father except through Me" (Jn. 14:6).

- A message about sin. Unbelievers must know that God has a holy standard for them to live by. They must hear their own sin condition and position in relation to God (Romans 3:23). They must hear that God is holy and righteous and separates Himself from sin and those in sin. They must hear that their sin can be and will be forgiven by accepting Jesus Christ as Savior.

- A message about the death issues of the unsaved is vital. Unbelievers must be guided and awakened to the reality that death, spiritual and physical, is real. There is death at the end of physical life and there is a spiritual death that separates man from God because of sin.

- A biblical message that produces faith in the unsaved person. The Word of God teaches, "So then faith comes by hearing and hearing by the Word of God" (Rom. 10:17) There must be a clear presentation of the Word of God to which the unbeliever can respond. It is critically important that the Word of God is presented in a manner that the unsaved will truly hear and understand His Word. As they hear His Word, it will bring faith into their lives.

- Repentance. As the Word of God is presented, it will bring conviction and repentance. The Word of God will move the unsaved to make decisions to turn and go in a new direction, accepting Jesus as Savior. As faith comes to their hearts, the unsaved respond and turn to Jesus Christ. At the same time, they turn from their old lives and old nature. They gain a new sense of direction for life through faith in Christ, which is key in repentance—a changed life going in a new direction, following Him.

- Danger of hell. For an unbeliever to be evangelized at the deepest level, he or she must be warned about the consequences of their spiritual separation from God. This warning will include the reality of the eternal danger of hell. Effective witnessing can easily include a sensitive introduction of the danger of hell and unbelievers want to know the truth about hell. Believers must warn gently with a biblical answer. Warn and teach through the effective presentation of the salvation gospel of Jesus Christ.

- A point of decision. The conclusion must be a clear invitation for the unsaved to receive Jesus Christ as Lord and Savior. A witnessing believer's role is to lead the unsaved by guiding them to simply receive Jesus Christ as Savior. Unbelievers must be sensitively confronted, taught, warned and given an opportunity to make their decision.

All of these powerful components, working together deeply evangelize an unbeliever. They are designed to warn unbelievers about the eternal danger of living without Christ. This soulwinning plan will equip believers to warn unbelievers of the danger they are in and then, almost effortlessly, lead them to eternal safety in Christ. The apostle Paul declared, "Him we preach, warning every man and teaching every man in all wisdom, that we may present every man perfect in Christ Jesus." (Col. 1:28)

Worried about the word *preach* or *preaching*? Don't be. Any believer can easily be trained to present the Word of God to an unbeliever. When the Word of God is presented and an unbeliever is asked to make a decision for Christ, that is preaching the gospel. The basic difference in preaching and teaching is that preaching calls for a decision. Anytime a believer shares or witnesses and asks for a decision, they are involved in a form of preaching. Do not confuse witnessing and winning souls with congregational preaching from a pulpit. You are not being trained or asked to do pulpit ministry. You are being equipped to present the Word of God through a soulwinning plan that includes asking unbelievers for a decision to pray to receive Jesus as Savior. That is a form of preaching on a personal level, and all of the components necessary to evangelize an unbeliever are in your soulwinning plan.

## THE WORD OF GOD IMPLODES
## WRONG THINKING OF THE UNSAVED

A witnessing exchange that includes all of the ten components just referred to will powerfully impact and evangelize unbelievers. There is no stronger impact upon an unbeliever than a clear, articulate, and understandable presentation of biblical truths and historical reality that will create a critical mass experience impacting the soul of an unbeliever. This critical mass of biblical truth and reality will impact, evangelize, and draw an unsaved person to Christ as Savior.

A critical mass experience in any situation is what is created when elements of many different dimensions come together and start interacting. The reaction result of a critical mass is that different elements coming together react and create a new dimension or set of circumstances. Critical mass experiences can generate a good change or a bad change in any particular situation. The critical mass and new change created through this soulwinning plan will be a born again believer.

The critical mass experience from various components of the plan causes an implosion of the unsaved soul because of the unique presentation of so much power and truth. That means their ungodly belief system will implode or collapse in the deepest recesses of their unsaved soul. Former belief systems will collapse when powerfully and strategically confronted with the claims of Christ in the Word of God and unbelievers come to Christ.

Throughout the plan the impact of a critical mass of strategic biblical truth is powerful and strongly evangelizes an unbeliever. Loosely held beliefs of unbelievers will be affected in a powerful way. Unstable belief systems will be shaken to the core of an unbeliever's soul as they are impacted by the glorious salvation gospel of Jesus Christ. They suddenly realize and know that previously held ideas and philosophies about God or eternal issues outside of Jesus Christ are unstable and unsupportable. The impact of the biblical critical mass experience will bring the unsaved person to the mindset of vulnerability and receptivity to the truth in His Word. The Word of God breaks down their unstable belief system and eliminates their resistance to Him.

> For though we walk in the flesh, we do not war according to the flesh. For the weapons of our warfare are not carnal but mighty in God for pulling down strongholds, casting down arguments and every high thing that exalts itself against the knowledge of God, bringing every thought into captivity to the obedience of Christ.
>
> —2 CORINTHIANS 10:3–5

## WITNESSING AND WINNING SOULS IS SPIRITUAL WARFARE

Witnessing and winning souls is spiritual warfare. Once witnessing is started there is a spiritual battle with a believer, in which the enemy is engaged for the soul of his captive. Believers may not realize that witnessing is war, but Satan does and he has most of the body of Christ convinced that they cannot win this spiritual war through witnessing.

The defensive and wrong beliefs held by the unsaved have been based mostly on myth, biblical heresy, self-works, self-delusion, new age concepts, astrology, or superstition. These are all easily identifiable points of untruth where Satan has a grip on unbelievers. When believers engage in witnessing they are directly assaulting the grip that Satan has on an unbeliever's life. An unbeliever may be well educated and outwardly a very nice person, but their worldly life philosophy is from Satan's invisible grip upon their soul.

## SATAN'S LIES TO UNBELIEVERS AND BELIEVERS

The lie of the devil will come against believers and unbelievers. Satan will not relinquish his grip without a fight. The lie of the devil to an unbeliever is they do not need Jesus Christ. The lie to the believer is they cannot win the unbeliever. Satan's lying spirit will tell believers *they cannot succeed, that unbelievers don't really want to hear what they have to say; they should give up on the unbeliever or why bother because the unbeliever won't listen anyway!* Satan is a deceiver and his lies can come in many ways and forms.

Winning souls is winning unbelievers away from the grip of Satan into the kingdom of God in Jesus Christ. When confronted with a sensitive and accurate presentation of the powerful words of God, Satan and an unbeliever will surrender. The Word of God will break Satan's grip, and the unbeliever will surrender to Jesus Christ as Savior. It is prayer, the power of the Holy Spirit, and the Word of God that brings down satanic strongholds, not your words or mine.

> The effective, fervent prayer of a righteous man avails much.
> —JAMES 5:16

The power in the Word of God will dismantle unbiblical belief systems and thinking. As the Word of God dismantles unbiblical beliefs and unbelievers are in the process of surrendering, you the believer can lead them to their place of total surrender, receiving Jesus Christ as Savior.

Finally, my brethren, be strong in the Lord and in the power of His might. Put on the whole armor of God, that you may be able to stand against the wiles of the devil. For we do not wrestle against flesh and blood, but against principalities, against powers, against the rulers of the darkness of this age, against spiritual hosts of wickedness in the heavenly places. Therefore take up the whole armor of God, that you may be able to withstand in the evil day, and having done all, to stand. Stand therefore, having girded your waist with truth, having put on the breastplate of righteousness, and having shod your feet with the preparation of the gospel of peace; above all, taking the shield of faith with which you will be able to quench all the fiery darts of the wicked one. And take the helmet of salvation, and the sword of the Spirit, being watchful to this end with all perseverance and supplication for all the saints—and for me, that utterance may be given to me, that I may open my mouth boldly to make known the mystery of the gospel.

—EPHESIANS 6:10–19

Believers can put on the whole armor of God by their personal confessing of being equipped to win souls with the *Witnessing Winzone* plan. With their positive confession of faith from being equipped with the soulwinning plan, believers will be powerfully equipped to stand, witness, and win souls to Jesus Christ.

## CONTROLLED AND UNCONTROLLED SITUATIONS

With your new soulwinning plan you will have an assurance and boldness to immediately witness and win souls. The most exciting news for believers is that with this soulwinning plan, you and the Holy Spirit can be in complete control of any witnessing exchange. Using wisdom as to what is going on around you, it is then that you introduce unbelievers to the gospel of Christ. It does not matter what environment you are in with the unbeliever that you want to win to Christ. What is imperative is that in the environment where you find yourself witnessing, you feel that you can proceed with winning the person to Christ without interruption.

At times you may need to change the environment location by simply inviting an unsaved person to join you and go somewhere else or take a simple walk together. You do not want to be interrupted in the midst of winning a soul to Christ. Controlled situations are those situations when you sense all is well and you can proceed uninterrupted. Uncontrolled situations are those situations when an interruption can occur and you sense most probably will occur. Be wise and use common sense concerning controlled and uncontrolled situations.

## SAVED IN A SORT OF SEMI-CONTROLLED ENVIRONMENT

A few years ago, I was a guest at a grandiose wedding and reception at the elite Bel-Air Country Club in Los Angeles, California. It was an opulent affair and former Judge Wopner of TV fame presided. I was seated next to the 50-plus-piece orchestra at the reception and seated to my right was the wealthy, eighty-year-old, former mother-in-law of the groom, a movie mogul. As it turned out the bride was a closet lesbian, intent on getting the groom's money. The marriage ended in three weeks. That's Hollywood, but back to the main story....As the evening went on, the former mother-in-law and I struck up a conversation and I shared with her that I was a Christian. She thought that was nice. In the midst of a lot of excitement swirling around us, I led her to Christ, using my soulwinning plan. While other guests were dancing, she and I held hands, bowed our heads toward each other, and I led her through her sinner's prayer. I led her to receive Jesus Christ as Savior in the middle of one the loudest dance numbers imaginable. Souls can be won anywhere, anytime, when you sense it is appropriate. The strategic plan that you are learning is precisely what I used to lead her to Jesus Christ as her Savior.

## YOUR TERMS OR THEIR TERMS

A witness exchange with an unbeliever will end in one of two ways: on the believer's terms or the unbeliever's terms. Here are three key challenging areas to overcome in order for the witness exchange to end on a believer's terms:

1. Even though Christians initiate witnessing exchanges, many times the unbeliever receiving the witness has control of the conversation. This results in a witness exchange with limited or minimal communication and a general lack of cooperative participation. The unsaved can stop the witnessing process anytime they please by simply stopping the conversation or just walking away. As a result, Christians feel that they are on the defensive because they have an inadequate concept of how to move forward with confidence. This is just one of the negatives in an unprepared witnessing exchange. This soulwinning plan completely reverses this problem by giving the witnessing believer the understanding of how to initiate the conversation whenever they feel the time is right in order to control the outcome.

2. Many times unsaved people are in a defensive posture with large barriers around themselves. These barriers are designed to prevent believers from getting too close and personal with what they truly think or believe. As a result of the defensive barriers unbelievers throw up, Christians are unsure of a clear direction for witnessing. They feel uncertain about exactly what is going on in the mind of the unsaved person. Many times after an unbeliever has been witnessed to, they simply walk away and believers have no idea why the unbeliever did not come to Christ.

3. Believers may be unsure in their own minds about the direction of their witnessing effort. They know that the goal needs to be for the unsaved person to receive Jesus

as Savior. The challenge is to present the gospel in a
way that the unsaved will follow along, see the need and
respond by praying to receive Christ. Insecurity on the
part of believer always becomes magnified when they are
unsure of what they are doing.

Without being equipped, witnessing under these circumstances
can become very scary and challenging. Believers can completely
overcome these challenges by equipping themselves with this soulwinning plan. One of the great values of this plan is that you will
be in control because you can direct witness exchanges where you
want them to go. You are no longer at the mercy of an unbeliever's
whims but are powerfully equipped to manage and lead any witnessing exchange.

## TRANSFORMED TO BE ON OFFENSE

Becoming thoroughly equipped to witness will completely reverse
any negative or defensive mindset you have had regarding soulwinning that comes from uncertainty in the witnessing process.
It will place a witnessing believer who wants to win souls on the
offense instead of the defense. You will not be on the offense in a
negative sense, but because you are self-assured of the clear direction in exactly how to win an unsaved person to Jesus Christ.
Being on the offense does not mean you are an offensive person.
It means you are released into being a self-assured and confident,
witnessing believer.

This confidence will come from an ability to take the witness
exchange forward to a soulwinning conclusion because of a clear
soulwinning path you have learned. A positive, on-the-offense
position is when a believer is convinced that there can actually be
a victory in a witness exchange. Believers will have confidence to
initiate the witness exchange because they will be assured that they
can win the exchange with this strategic plan.

After you learn your plan, the goal in typically casual witnessing will be for you to lead witness exchanges toward the beginning

97

of the plan's strategy. Because there is now a specific soulwinning closure plan, believers now have a specific direction to lead all witnessing exchanges toward that end.

## NEWFOUND FAITH
## AND ASSURANCE TO WIN SOULS

The gospel of Matthew records the story of a Roman centurion. This centurion walked by faith whether he knew it or not. The scriptures declare:

> Now when Jesus had entered Capernaum, a centurion came to Him, pleading with Him saying, 'Lord, my servant is lying at home paralyzed, dreadfully tormented.' And Jesus said to him, 'I will come and heal him.' The centurion answered and said, 'Lord, I am not worthy that You should come under my roof. But only speak a word, and my servant will be healed. For I also am a man under authority, having soldiers under me. And I say to this one, 'Go,' and he goes; and to another, 'Come,' and he comes; and to my servant, 'Do this,' and he does it.' When Jesus heard it, He marveled, and said to those who followed, 'Assuredly, I say to you, I have not found such great faith, not even in Israel!'
>
> —MATTHEW 8:5–8

When Jesus heard the centurion explain that He did not have to come to his home to heal his servant, He was mightily impressed! He declared: "Assuredly, I say to you, I have not found such great faith, not even in Israel!" (Matt. 8:10). Jesus said that about the centurion because He realized the centurion understood the power of living a life under authority. There was a personal reality attached to what the centurion believed about Jesus and what He could do.

After mastering the *Witnessing Winzone* strategy for winning souls, you will develop a newfound faith and boldness to win souls as powerful as the faith of that centurion. Any believer can develop a strong and successful foundation for a faith-based assurance to deal with any witnessing or soulwinning experience with solid confidence. What will be a remarkable change for believers will be that their personal prayer question will not be *Lord, who do you want me to witness to?* The personal prayer question will be *Lord, who you want me to win?*

The centurion's faith was rooted in what he understood about authority out of his own experience, and he recognized and understood the authority and power that Jesus had in His ministry. The centurion related the power and authority that Jesus had to his own situation and his faith in Jesus was doubtless. Centurion-type faith is a doubtless belief in Jesus Christ and His authority and power.

As you become equipped to win souls, you will develop a centurion-type faith in Jesus, the Word of God, and your newfound ability to successfully witness in any situation.

## ETERNITY IS A LONG FLIGHT

Eternal separation from God is the destination of all unsaved humanity. This is as a result of sin and is the ultimate manifestation of God's wrath. Millions of souls are trapped today in drugs, alcohol and crime, and are in the grip of Satan's lies. They are living a hellish life on earth, because of a life in sin. Millions of unsaved men, women, boys and girls, on the surface, appear to be living out successful and normal lives. The reality is that no matter how wonderful their social, business or academic veneer appears, millions are in sin and need salvation. The unsaved face a tragic eternity too horrifying to fully grasp or imagine after physical death occurs. The unsaved who did not know God in this life will not know Him in eternal life. Millions are already suffering in agony in hell. But that is not God's plan: "But God demonstrates His own love toward us, in that while we were sinners, Christ died for us. Much more then, having now been justified by His blood, we shall be saved from wrath through Him. (Rom. 5:8–9).

After death, nothing can be done about lost souls being in hell.

How long is forever, everlasting or eternity? For Christians, eternity in Christ is the promise of everlasting glory and joy. For the unsaved, hell is a horrible scenario that is also everlasting. Here is a simple story about a little sparrow that helps give some perspective to eternity:

> There once was a little sparrow and he was commanded to go first to beaches and then deserts. When in those places he was to take a grain of sand in his beak and fly to the moon. Upon arriving on the moon, he would deposit the grain of sand on the surface of the moon. After he did that, he was to fly back to earth and get another grain of sand and continue doing that until he transferred all the sand upon the earth to the moon.
>
> The moon is approximately 250,000 miles from earth. A sparrow flies at approximately 40 miles per hour. Flying 24 hours a day one round trip after depositing one grain of sand will take approximately 1 year and 5 months. Finally, after every grain of sand is taken from all the beaches and deserts around the world, after millions of years of flying back and forth and every grain of sand is individually deposited on the moon's surface, eternity will have just begun.

Those in Christ can look forward to an eternity of glory in the presence of the Lord. Unbelievers face an eternity of separation, horror and disaster in hell. Christians must fully awaken to the enormity of the tragedy of lost souls. We in Christ have the only solution to the problem for the millions of unsaved people who are still alive. Jesus is coming again. Now is the time to become equipped to lead unbelievers into salvation in Him. Jesus declared, "But I will show you whom you should fear: Fear Him who after He has killed, has power to cast into hell; yes, I say to you, fear Him!" (Luke 12:5).

The only hell a believer will ever experience is any hell that they experience in this life. The only heaven an unbeliever will ever experience is whatever heaven they experience in this life.

# Jesus' Mindset on Sowing and Reaping

I N THE FOURTH CHAPTER OF John, there is an exciting and
revealing story about Jesus and the Samaritan woman at the
well. After Jesus revealed to the woman that He indeed was
the hoped-for Messiah, she became excited and went back to her
community telling everyone she could that she had found the
Messiah. This story gives an insightful look at the heart of Jesus
and His teaching about sowing and reaping. In doing so He offers
and promotes a *wage* reward for those who do. He clearly identifies
His emphasis on reaping and states that reaping is available now.
Reaping is not a deferred process, but is for now! In His discourse
He mentions that a *wage* is only for reapers, not for sowers. In the
John 4 text He refers to three exciting events identified with reap-
ers and one with sowers:

> In the meantime His disciples urged Him, saying, 'Rabbi, eat.'
> But He said to them, 'I have food to eat of which you do not
> know.' Therefore the disciples said to one another, 'Has any-
> one brought Him anything to eat?' Jesus said to them, 'My
> food is to do the will of Him who sent Me, and to finish His
> work. Do you not say, 'There are still four months and then
> comes the harvest?' Behold, I say to you, lift up your eyes and
> look at the fields, for they are already white for harvest! And
> he who reaps receives wages, and gathers fruit for eternal life,

that both he who sows and he who reaps may rejoice together. For in this the saying is true: 'One sows and another reaps.' I sent you to reap that for which you have not labored; others have labored, and you have entered into their labors.'

—JOHN 4:31–38

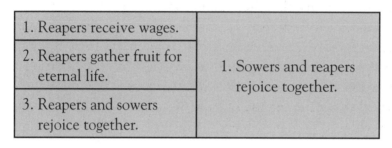

| 1. Reapers receive wages. | |
| 2. Reapers gather fruit for eternal life. | 1. Sowers and reapers rejoice together. |
| 3. Reapers and sowers rejoice together. | |

He is strongly encouraging believers to have a mindset of immediate reaping or winning souls instead of a postponement mindset from a focus on sowing or witnessing. He does not say *do not sow* as He knew that there would always be those who focus on sowing. He is clarifying His will and purpose for believers to be focused on reaping. Jesus is promoting reaping and winning souls and to approach reaping with the attitude that a sowing work has already been done.

Even though He identifies reapers as those who win souls and gain a wage, He also refers to a unity of purpose with sowers and reapers.

And he who reaps receives wages, and gathers fruit for eternal life, that both he who sows and he who reaps may rejoice together. For in this the saying is true: 'One sows and another reaps.' I sent you to reap that for which you have not labored; others have labored, and you have entered into their labors."

—JOHN 4:16–37

Sowers get excited, just as those who reap, when they hear souls are won. They are both thrilled and rejoice together when anyone is saved. Winning souls is not about a divisive contest between sowers and reapers. As real as rewards are, and a wage is some form of reward, He is using them to highlight His priority in evangelistic outreach. Earlier in the text He encourages believers to be stretched and do more than sow, but knows some are only going to do what they feel they are capable of doing in personal evangelism. Believers can now realign their thinking with His because with this soulwinning plan they can become equipped to reap.

His idea is to be prepared to reap because when they are equipped and prepared, they are automatically equipped to do both. Different personal evangelism opportunities will always arise, whether sowing or reaping. If a believer is willing to witness but not equipped to reap, they are limited to only sow. Why be limited? Get equipped, win souls, and receive a reaper's wage reward.

> And he who wins souls is wise.
>
> —PROVERBS 11:30

Another scripture that refers to rewards and a unity of purpose and cooperation is from Paul's letter to the Corinthian church. It does not refer to a reward as emphatically as Jesus did the wage for reaping. Whatever a reward is or a wage is, they are real and it is exciting and glorious to know that they are from our Lord, Jesus Christ.

> And I, brethren, could not speak to you as to spiritual people but as to carnal, as to babes in Christ. I fed you with milk and not with sold food; for until now you were not able to receive it; for you are still carnal. For where there are envy, strife, and divisions among you, are you not carnal and behaving like mere men? For when one says, "I am of Paul," and another, "I am of Apollos," are you not carnal? Who then is Paul, and who is Apollos, but ministers through whom you believed, as the Lord gave to each one? I planted, Apollos watered, but God gave the increase. Now he who plants and he who waters are one, and each one will receive his own reward according to his own labor.
>
> —1 CORINTHIANS 3:1–8

Paul is addressing Corinthian church members who were divided over supporting different teachers and leaders. In trying to stop local fussing over whom they should follow and listen to, either Paul or Apollos, he points out an immaturity in local believers. He is telling the Corinthian church members to not argue about which leader to follow like the world would do. His focus is on a cooperative spirit because leaders cooperatively do their part to build the church. In Paul's case, he was an apostle, author, traveling evangelist/soulwinner, church planter, and teacher. Apollos, according to Acts 18:25, "taught accurately the things of the Lord," traveled to Corinth, and was now a local teacher who watered or fed the flock. Paul is trying to get the Corinthians to stop fighting over them as they will both do their own work and will get their own reward. These appear to be ministry rewards other than a reaper's reward.

> Then He said to His disciples, "The harvest truly is plentiful, but the laborers are few. Therefore pray the Lord of the harvest to send out laborers into His harvest."
> —MATTHEW 9:37–38

Pray for souls to be won. These will include family members, friends, work associates, and others that need salvation. Get equipped to win and pray to win those you have the opportunity to win. Believers pray for many issues that impact their lives, and praying for the lost souls they can reach will also be heard and blessed. Pray for a reaper's blessing and a reaper's opportunity. Do not worry about sowing because once you are equipped sowing naturally takes place

> The effective, fervent prayer of a righteous man avails much.
> —JAMES 5:16

## REAPERS SOW AND REAP

If your goal is going to be to reap, you first have to know how to reap. If sowing is the goal, all you will do is sow. In the process of reaping, you will always sow. A believer always sows when they reap. It is a built in part of the reaping dynamic. A reaper will both sow and reap. A sower only sows, because if sowing is a goal, it is an end in itself. That means it is left for another to do the reaping. This biblical soulwinning plan makes it easy to accomplish both sowing and reaping at the same time. Everything is built into the plan. For those who have felt they only want to sow, they can, and by taking a small extra step, they can reap as well. Jesus sends us to reap and that must be our goal in personal evangelism. The ability to reap is the ability to win souls and feeling assured that you have the ability to reap when the opportunity presents itself.

It is rare with this plan, but if in the attempt to reap there is no salvation decision, the unsaved person will still have heard a clear and powerful biblical presentation. The unbeliever will have heard as clear a presentation of the salvation gospel of Jesus Christ as they could possibly hear. They will not forget the Word of God and the Holy Spirit will not let them forget. When you know how to win souls, you have become a reaper and have unlimited potential to be used of God.

## Sowing Without Reaping Is Dangerous

Incomplete witnessing/sowing can be extremely dangerous. How many have been witnessed to, not won to Christ, and end up in a cult, some New Age movement or one of the Eastern mysticism religions? There are unsaved seekers out there who want to know the truth. They do not know what the truth is but would like to find it or at least think they want to find it. The role of effective witnessing is to lead them into the truth. Just talking about the truth is not enough. The unsaved must be led or guided into the truth, which means leading them to receive Jesus as Savior.

The goal of witnessing is to win souls, not whet appetites about the things of God without satisfying those appetites. If an unbeliever is given enough to hunger for more through your witness, where are they going to get the more? These are questions that individual believers must wrestle with and make personal decisions about getting equipped to win souls. Believers must be equipped to satisfy those hunger-for-God appetites aroused in unbelievers.

Believers, just like you, are always around unbelievers who are being influenced by a combination of cults and false religions. Many of these unbelievers are genuine seekers who have already been reaped or are in the process of being reaped by the wrong crowd. You can make an immediate difference because now you can win many of these potential cult victims to Jesus Christ as Savior.

As a result of an unstructured witness about Jesus, all an unprepared witnessing believer can do is just hope for the best and many times see the worst happen. Dr. Jack Van Impe Ministries estimates that over 70 percent of all people trapped in cults have been witnessed to, or have been to a church or been part of a church.

An unsaved person is already in eternal danger. They will remain in eternal danger unless the witnessing concludes with the lost person praying to receive Jesus as Savior. That unsaved person can have their interest in the things of God stirred up and out of ignorance end up being won into a cult or some New Age religion. Believers must never confuse sowing with reaping and believe that everyone that they witness to will end up in the kingdom of God.

The church is in a competitive war for souls. Islam wants to reap. Scientology wants to reap. Buddhism wants to reap. Unification Church wants to reap. The Church of the Latter Day Saints wants to reap. Eastern mysticism and the New Age Religions want to reap. The list of false religions goes on and on. When a false religion reaps a soul, that false religion is solidifying Satan's grip on the soul that is already under his control. Satan is behind every false religion and they are all sowing, reaping and discipling in the same places where believers live. 1 Pet 5:8 declares:

> Be sober; be vigilant; because your adversary the devil walks about like a roaring lion, seeking whom he may devour.

## IF BELIEVERS DON'T, OTHERS WILL

A story is told about a Christian man who commuted to a distant part of the city to his place of employment. At work he knew he should be a good example. He felt he shouldn't impose upon others by actively witnessing and felt secure being a *silent witness*. He wanted to let his consistent and good work speak for who he was in Christ. He lived and went to church about thirty miles from where he worked and was convinced that if he won someone to Christ they would never come to his church anyway. He lived and worked with this approach to witnessing silently for many years.

One day a co-worker came up to him just filled with joy and said to the Christian man, "You have been a wonderful example to me. You were always polite and did a good job and tried to help others. I know that you are a good and religious Christian man." The co-worker went on to say, "Some other men here really started talking to me and working on me to get right with God. Because I respect you so much, I wanted you to know I am thrilled to have found God. I am so happy and love going to the Kingdom Hall with my new brothers and sisters in my Jehovah's Witnesses family. Thank you for being such a good example and role model for me." Things like this happen every day! With your new soulwinning plan it is now easy to get equipped and not hesitate to reach out to unbelievers anywhere.

## THE GREATEST HARVEST
## WILL NOT BE REAPED FROM PULPITS

Thousands of pastors and evangelists in pulpits and media outlets are winning souls to Jesus Christ. These great pastors and evangelists are doing a tremendous work. Yet, the potential for the greatest soulwinning harvest of history can come from the millions of believers in the body of Christ who have been equipped to win souls. These same newly equipped, precious saints can and will make an unbelievable soulwinning impact on the "mission fields" of where they live, work and play. Witnessing and winning souls in personal evangelism can be the most powerful front line attack in God's plan to win and disciple the world.

A harvest is waiting for those who are willing to get equipped to enter into the harvest and to become harvesters. Harvesters are soulwinners, and like any other type of worker, they have to be trained. Now is the time to begin praying and developing commitments about how to be used in His harvest. As you learn how to win souls, begin praying for unsaved souls. Start praying for those who are unsaved in your families, work places and the areas of life that you frequent. Begin praying for lost souls right now, and after you are equipped, opportunities to win souls will seem to come out of nowhere. In Luke 10:2 the Bible says:

> Then He said to them, 'The harvest truly is great, but the laborers are few; therefore pray the Lord of the harvest to send out laborers into His harvest.'

## WHAT DOES "SHARE YOUR FAITH" REALLY MEAN?

When believers are told to go share their faith, they are told to do so based upon some traditional assumptions. One simple assumption is that since believers know Jesus Christ as Savior, they should be able to convince an unbeliever of the need for them to have Him as their own Savior. Another simple assumption is that since believers know the truth, they should automatically be able to convince an unbeliever of the truth they know. Unfortunately, it rarely works that way.

What does the phrase *share your faith* mean to you? This is a witnessing challenge that all believers face. Believers are told to do what they have not been trained to do. And many feel very uncertain about what *share your faith* means. Many in the body of Christ assume everyone understands what this phrase means. Unfortunately, the implications in the phrase *share your faith* are so broad that it is difficult to define it in one precise statement. The reality is that it is turns out to mean for many primarily a sowing process. The underlying goal is to win souls, but with no direction or training in the process, souls are rarely won in personal evangelism by those who simply try to share their faith.

When believers are told to *share their faith*, a few logical questions are, *how do I do it, how much and which part or where do I start?* A believer has a lot to share about Jesus Christ and what He can mean in any person's life. They know that they are the salt of the earth and they are to let their light shine. Believers can share how much He has blessed them. There are no limitations as to how much Jesus can touch a life and there is much to know, love and share about Jesus Christ. When some believers hear *go and share your faith,* they translate that into *go and share your personal testimony.* In that way, many are limited to do only "testimony witnessing." To *share your faith* may include some personal testimony, but substantially it is to share the claims of the cross, as we have explained. It means to explain why and what Christ came to do through His birth, His death, burial and resurrection. Without thoughtful planning it is an overwhelming challenge to do so effectively and consistently.

> For God so loved the world that He gave His only begotten Son, that whoever believes in Him should not perish but have everlasting life.
>
> —JOHN 3:16

> Jesus said to him, "I am the way, the truth, and the life. No one comes to the Father except through Me.
>
> —JOHN 14:6

Through many personal evangelism experiences and discussions with other believers, I have come to the conclusion that there is no clear universal understanding of what it means to *share your faith*. I believe there are many assumptions about what this means, but not clear understanding. This traditional personal evangelism exhortation can mean many things to many different believers. The implication in the exhortation is that believers already know what *share your faith* means and how to go about it. It also seems to imply to *share your faith or at least what you know or think you can*. Millions of believers have heart-felt desires to witness and win souls. Yet, they find that instead of feeling confident, they are confronted with an avalanche of unanswered questions and concerns that brings them to a total standstill due to fear and confusion.

## GET PAST INTIMIDATION IN WITNESSING AND WINNING SOULS

In general witnessing and/or personal testimony many believers are engaged in dialogues with no clear direction, therefore no control, that leads to a salvation conclusion. Believers are at the mercy of unbelievers' unknown reactions as they share their faith. Without being equipped, entering into these kinds of witnessing conversations can be quite intimidating for anyone. The strategy of the soulwinning plan leads unbelievers into the type of witnessing conversation that believers know has a clear direction that will lead to a salvation conclusion. That is the kind of assurance and personal control that will completely eliminate fear and intimidation in *sharing your faith* and winning souls.

If you are like I was, until now you may not have had the opportunity to hear an evangelistic strategy and discover that winning souls can be quite simple. Like most believers, I was told that to be a good Christian I should witness or *share my faith* and win souls—but all these concepts were a bit hazy for me. All of that quickly changed when I was first introduced to the concept of a basic, planned gospel presentation. This is a powerful, breakthrough, soulwinning model because of its clarity and unique method of presenting the claims of Christ in the Word of God. Any believer can now become fully equipped to win souls through this exciting plan that gives you a precise roadmap through the soulwinning process.

## WITNESSING WITH NO
## STRATEGY WILL BE A LOSING BATTLE

Believers who are told to *just go and share your faith* are being encouraged to engage an unsaved person in a general conversation explaining why they believe in Jesus Christ. It is a traditional witnessing exhortation that is too broad and general, with no closure built into the process. It sounds comfortable and uncomplicated, but in reality, without structure and planning it is not. Learning the soulwinning plan will equip and take you beyond the frustration of the traditional witnessing exhortation to *just go and share your faith*. Believers have a lot of faith to share. The basic problem is there is not a specific beginning or end, when told to *just share your faith*. Most believers just don't know exactly where to start much less where to stop. That is why so many witnessing dialogues end with no specificity or focused closure and believers end up frustrated and disheartened.

If there is no specific strategy, witnessing can become directionless. How many times have believers walked away from spirited and exciting witnessing exchanges thinking, *I wish I had said this or that*. How many times have believers walked away from an unsaved person wondering, what went wrong, or worse, feeling guilt ridden with *what did I do wrong?* The great tragedy for millions of believers is that out of frustration they have given up all attempts to witness, much less win souls. After you learn to implement your new soulwinning plan, you will never have to deal with the many frustrating issues that intimidate so many believers. You will be successful in winning souls and will only want to go forward and win more and more to Jesus Christ.

Most experienced soulwinners generally have found or developed some form of an evangelistic style or technique that is a strategy in their own minds. They may not actually identify what they do as strategic but somewhere in their thinking they have a concept that directs their witnessing. Any concept that directs a witness exchange is a strategy. The question then becomes how much of a strategy do they use in witnessing? For some believers, a minimal strategy is all that is necessary to point them to a soul-winning result. The important factor in this plan is that it guides believers towards a soulwinning conclusion.

## YOUR SOULWINNING PROBLEMS ARE SOLVED!

The traditional evangelism exhortation to *share your faith* implies that believers have to develop their own personal strategy for witnessing and winning souls. That is exactly what I was told at the conclusion of a Bible College evangelism course many years ago. With the *Witnessing Winzone* soulwinning plan you do not need to develop anything; it is already developed for you. It is biblical, strategic, and easy to learn and use, adapting it to your own personality. It completely solves the main problem that believers struggle with, which is simply to know what to say, when to say it, and how to say it in a witness exchange.

One of the most common, but very solvable problems in witness exchanges, is that many witnessing believers start telling unbelievers about Jesus before these unbelievers are ready to hear about Him. As a result, many times there is an overzealous or unfocused witnessing that unbelievers are completely unprepared to hear or receive. Believers want to share their faith—they have been encouraged to share their faith—and many times are intent on sharing their faith, no matter what. Believers can get frustrated and sometimes are over-aggressive when telling an unbeliever about Jesus, simply because they want to tell about Him. An unbeliever may not be ready to receive and can easily end up turned off to both the witnessing believer and to Jesus. There are many hurting unbelievers who have been mishandled by believers. I think that most of us, myself included, can remember an argument or a negative encounter with an unbeliever that we wish we could take back.

As you learn to use your new soulwinning plan, asking strategic questions to allow an unbeliever to think about eternal issues, you will discover it completely solves these problems. It gives you the way to biblically and strategically, yet sensitively, share your faith in a way that leads to salvation conclusions.

In its simplest form, "sharing your faith" relates to any witnessing conversation with an unbeliever about things appropriate to the conversation that a believer knows about Jesus Christ. A sharing-your-faith conversation generally attempts to engage, encourage, and lead an unbeliever to his or her own decision to receive Jesus Christ as Savior.

The main problems that the *Witnessing Winzone* soulwinning plan solves when sharing your faith are:

- The plan completely solves the fear problem from the unknown factor of what to say to believers during typical witnessing exchanges.

- The plan can create receptivity to the salvation gospel of Jesus Christ even when sharing your faith is unstructured.

- The process of witnessing may be unstructured, but the plan gives it a structure because it has a direction towards leading an unbeliever to a decision for Christ.

- Believers are free to comfortably share whatever they want about their faith because of the concluding, soulwinning direction to always take a witnessing dialogue.

Without an effective way to conclude or close a witnessing exchange or a share-your-faith exchange, the process becomes loose ended and unbelievers drift away spiritually and emotionally unfulfilled. They are unfulfilled because they listened to a believer share his faith, know the believer is fulfilled in his belief, but unless the unbeliever comes to Jesus Christ he will be unfulfilled in the process. Unbelievers want Jesus Christ. Believers must give Him to them in a way that they can receive Him.

Some believers must have a greater witnessing goal than a

self-satisfactory "I just told him!" or "I just told her!" and then feel they did their witnessing "duty." If an unbeliever is unfulfilled as a result of weak or abusive witnessing there are plenty of ungodly religious groups ready, willing, and able to offer them a deceptive fulfillment. The way an unbeliever is spiritually and emotionally fulfilled is by clearly hearing the salvation gospel and responding to Jesus Christ as Savior.

## ATHLETIC COMPARISONS ARE BIBLICAL

The Apostle Paul liked athletic illustrations and he wrote about them. Paul wrote about runners on some occasions and about a boxer on another. The following text is an athletic metaphor about achieving and living a life in Christ as if it were a race for a prize. Paul is encouraging all Christians to run the race of life in Christ like a competition and to make an effort to win the prize:

> Do you not know that those who run in a race all run, but one receives the prize? Run in such a way that you may obtain it. And everyone who competes for the prize is temperate in all things. Now they do it to obtain a perishable crown, but we for an imperishable crown. Therefore I run thus: not with uncertainty. Thus I fight: not as one who beats the air. But I discipline my body and bring it into subjection, lest, when I have preached to others, I myself should become disqualified.
> — 1 CORINTHIANS 9:24–26

The apostle Paul is exhorting believers to get focused and have a mindset to win. There is a key statement in verse 26: "Therefore I run thus: not with uncertainty." Men and women of God are not called to be uncertain of a life in Christ. Believers should also not be uncertain about how to witness the salvation gospel. The exciting revelation for believers who have learned the *Witnessing Winzone* plan is that they will never again be uncertain in personal evangelism.

It is difficult for anyone to effectively compete in anything if filled with uncertainty. Scripture is telling believers to get focused, get equipped, pursue their potential and go for the prize. Exercising and learning their craft equips athletes to win. This is your new plan and it will get you and other believers in shape as soulwinners. Many great athletes say that during the greatest days of their lives in the competitive arena, they found themselves in a *zone* where it seemed they could not be stopped. Like great athletes, you too will discover that *zone* for witnessing in which you cannot be stopped short of the goal.

> It is not the will to win that is most important. It is the will to prepare to win that is most important.
> —BASKETBALL COACH BOBBY KNIGHT

## ATHLETES HAVE A ZONE— BELIEVERS HAVE A WINZONE!

Just like an athlete excels in the competition zone, you now have a soulwinning winzone that you can enter into, taking an unsaved person with you. This plan is now yours to use effectively, from the beginning, to the middle, and the closing decision for salvation. This unique plan is for believers to win witnessing exchanges, not lose them. No matter how anyone categorizes or rationalizes it, without a soulwinning plan, soulwinning opportunities slip away. Typical witnessing may include biblical references or contain some of your own personal testimony. It may include some back-and-forth questions and answers about what you or an unbeliever generally believes. General witnessing can also include some basic statements that the unsaved person wants to express to you. You may want to make some general statements that you want the unsaved person to hear. General witnessing will have its own conversational flow that cannot be scripted.

A sacred moment will begin when, under the leading of the Holy Spirit, you sense this is the moment to win the unbeliever to Christ. This is the time to stop typical and vague witnessing and begin to lead the unsaved person into your soulwinning plan.

When you learn this simple soulwinning plan so well that you do not stumble or stutter, you will be able to seize the sacred moments and consistently win unbelievers to Christ. The close or conclusion of the sacred moment is then you have prayed with the unsaved person to receive Christ. The next challenge is to encourage the new believer towards discipleship. Believers can reach out and develop relationships with unbelievers, but there always comes a moment of truth. That moment of truth is when a believer must lead or attempt to lead an unbeliever in a way that helps the unbeliever to say *yes* to Jesus Christ.

Because you now have a clear and precise soulwinning plan, unbelievers will perceive you as a solid man or woman of God. This is a subtle but important point because many unsaved people look for loose threads to unravel your Christian position or testimony. As a result of knowing what you are talking about, you will be perceived as a person in whom they can have confidence. The great thing about having a solidly planned presentation is that you always know where you are in the process and where you want to end up.

## WHAT KIND OF TEAM IS THIS?

Imagine a football team called the Christian Soldiers. The coach calls the team together to encourage them and give them their goal. Men, there are eleven of you and we need you to score touchdowns. There is the field and here is the ball, and you know what we need to do. Unfortunately, there are no designed plays for you. You have the overall picture and idea, so just make it up as you go. Trust God, do your best and go for it! Throughout the body of Christ, believers face this kind of scary scenario in personal evangelism. Is anyone really shocked that 90 percent of all believers have never won a single soul to Jesus Christ?

# 7

# Sensitive Witnessing Challenges

## FULFILLED LIVES IN CHRIST

BELIEVERS EVERYWHERE WANT TO LIVE in God's will and enjoy a life of fulfillment in Christ. The apostle Paul relates God's will and potential fulfillment for believers to doing the work of an evangelist, which connects to living a fulfilled life in Jesus Christ. While it is written to Timothy, it is encouraging and is for all believers:

> But you be watchful in all things, endure afflictions, do the work of an evangelist, fulfill your ministry.
>
> — 2 TIMOTHY 4:5

If you are praying and seeking God's will for your life and desire to fulfill your ministry, start winning souls. Soulwinners are ordinary believers just like you and me. The only thing that separates soulwinners from most believers is that somewhere along the way they learned to win souls, as you are now learning to do. These soulwinners learned style or technique to lead typical/casual witnessing exchanges into witnessing exchanges with salvation results. It is very important for believers to be aware of various subtleties that can take place based on the witnessing focus and conversation. The following are some sensitive, challenging points to be aware of when witnessing to unbelievers. They are points to be aware of that can potentially limit witnessing success.

- Is the witnessing focus on Jesus or on me?

- Do unbelievers have the same problems as you have?

- Do unbelievers really want to be like you?

- Are you limited to witnessing to the emotionally distraught?

- Is expressing personal zeal and emotion the answer to successful witnessing?

- Are untrained new believers the answer to successful witnessing?

These simple points are raised to create awareness to potential problems when witnessing is not focused on or does not include the salvation gospel of Jesus Christ. Unbelievers have many problems and challenges in their lives. A challenge for believers is not to be drawn into the problems of the unbeliever and limit witnessing to what unbelievers feel is most important to them. It is important to meet unbelievers at their point of *felt need*. A felt need is the immediate emotional or practical problem that an unbeliever is experiencing. An unbeliever's felt needs are open doors for witnessing opportunity. To relate to an unbeliever's felt need is important. The witnessing goal is to be able to help unbelievers in whatever need or spiritual condition they are in and to help them fully understand the claims of the cross. It is important to meet unbelievers wherever they are in life, but with this plan to share what Jesus can do at the greatest need of life. The greatest needs of life always lead to the cross of Jesus Christ. No matter what is going on in the life of an unbeliever, helping him or her must be balanced with presenting the claims of the cross. This plan gives you the ability to weave that glorious message into whatever witnessing focus is in process.

# Is the Witnessing
# Focus on Jesus or on Me?

The phrase, *"share your faith,"* as we have discussed, to many believers simply means sharing what Jesus has done in their lives. In this way, they focus on the *me* factor in personal testimony witnessing. The problem in only sharing or limiting sharing to personal experience is that it can come across like the witnessing believers are actually focusing on themselves. It is easy to give an impression that Jesus is just another problem solver rather than Savior. Some believers limit their presentation of Jesus to just the things that He has helped them through.

This limited kind of witnessing can sound like this: there may have been an emotional crisis and He helped *me*. There may have been a work problem and He helped *me*; a drinking or drug addiction problem and He helped *me*; a confusion issue and He helped *me*; a relational situation and He helped *me*. He has gotten *me* to where I am today or He has helped *me* to better focus on this or that.

A potentially hidden point of confusion for an unbeliever comes when a believer's witness is limited to personal testimony. If a believer's witnessing focus is that Jesus Christ has made *me* who I am today, Jesus can sound like just another alternative to any other self-help guru. The problem with focusing only on solving personal problems is that it is easy for an unbeliever to think, *I don't have that many problems or that particular kind of problem, so I don't need Jesus as much as you do.*

Believers know more about their own experience in Christ than anything else about Christ. It is easy to talk about Jesus and "me" and limit personal evangelism to that subject. A breakthrough for believers is realizing that unbelievers are far more interested in Jesus and "themselves" than they are in Jesus and "you." Unbelievers have to think about two people when believers focus their witnessing on personal testimony. They have to think about a witnessing believer and Jesus as Savior. If they can't trust one, they can't trust the other. In witnessing, it is better to keep most of the focus on the One they can absolutely trust, Jesus our Lord. If unbelievers have to make multiple decisions about more than one person it can add an unnecessary burden to their decision process. Witnessing that focuses on the claims of Christ helps to uncomplicate an unbeliever's decision to receive Jesus as Savior.

## Do Unbelievers Have the Same Problems As You?

The focus of witnessing should not be about believers and their problems. The problem with emphasizing Jesus Christ as a problem solver or emotional healer is that most people will not have the same problems and issues as you. They may not relate to your *personal testimony*. Your own personal testimony about receiving Jesus as Savior and all He has done for you may be the most important story of your life. To an unbeliever you can easily be just another problem person that found answers in a problem-solving *religious experience*. Witnessing Christians must learn to greatly reduce, and many times eliminate, the Me factor or problem-solving factor in witnessing. All sorts of worldly self-help gurus claim they have the answer to all sorts of problems. A believer's mission is not to prove that Jesus is a better self-help guru than whoever is the current champion of worldly self-improvement. This is exactly why this soulwinning plan focuses on the eternal danger issues of life.

## Do Unbelievers Really Want to Be Like You?

Sharing about Jesus as primarily a personal life changer or problem solver can create another subtle but potentially serious problem. Because there are many ways a person can merely *change* his or her life, communicating about Christ in this limited context can potentially raise a serious stumbling block for the unbeliever. An unspoken question can develop in the mind of the person being witnessed to, such as, *If Jesus has done all this for you and made you who you are, will I be like you? Or, If I accept Jesus and He helps me with my problems and changes me, do I want to be like you?* For some unsaved people, to become like you might seem like a plus; for others, to become like you might seem like a minus. Effective witnessing that leads to soulwinning results focuses on Jesus Christ, not believers.

When believers focus their witnessing on their personal testimonies, they are in reality holding themselves up as models of what Jesus Christ can do in a life. That can be a very sensitive witnessing proposition. Unbelievers can misunderstand it as a statement of *just look at me and see what Jesus can do in a life.* Believers are role models or at least should be good examples. At the same time, believers cannot assume that unbelievers automatically want to become like them. Unbelievers should certainly recognize something good and different in a believer, but at the same time, a witnessing believer may not be the current role model in the life of an unsaved person. Believers must be prepared to sensitively discuss the wonderful things Jesus Christ has done in their lives but be more prepared to effectively present the salvation message of the cross. What unbelievers really want that believers have is salvation in Jesus Christ. An unbeliever may appreciate how a believer lives his life and that is all on the external. They don't know it but what an unbeliever truly wants and needs is the Christ in the believer that makes the believer such a quality person. This involves letting unbelievers clearly know that all individuals have a sin problem that creates other problems and is only solved by receiving Jesus Christ as Savior.

## WITNESSING SHOULD BE
## CHRIST CENTERED, NOT YOU CENTERED

Witnessing challenges are all easily resolved by using your new plan and using it at every opportunity. The answer is for believers to have the ability to transition from self-focused personal testimony to the salvation gospel of Jesus Christ. In witnessing there is often a place for a sensitive and uplifting personal testimony. Unfortunately, if that is all a believer has to rely upon, their consistent success in winning souls will be quite limited. I rarely share my personal testimony, because I do not rely on it to win souls. Occasionally I do share my testimony, but only partially and when I feel it lends itself to the goal of winning a particular unbeliever. I only use parts of my personal testimony to lead to introducing this soulwinning plan, just like you will. If you let this soulwinning plan become foundational in all witnessing encounters, you will discover an ability to adapt and adjust to any set of witnessing circumstances. As you do, you will find the need to rely on self-focused testimony will diminish and your soulwinning results will explode!

## LIMITED TO WITNESSING TO THE EMOTIONALLY DISTRAUGHT?

Many believers feel most comfortable witnessing to an unsaved person who is emotionally distraught. There seems to be a sense of personal assurance for believers that are around unsaved people who are in emotional turmoil. A person in emotional crisis is extremely vulnerable. For some believers these types of personalities and conditions are the only situations where they personally feel comfortable witnessing. Some believers may feel secure and less vulnerable in these conditions only because the unsaved person is in emotional chaos and far more vulnerable. Perhaps this is just human nature, but your new soulwinning plan will free you to do much more and win more people to Christ. Believers should minister to and witness to unbelievers in emotional crisis. Of course, believers can now get past only feeling secure by witnessing to someone who is emotionally distraught.

This plan will get any believer past feeling they can only witness under these kinds of situations. It will take a believer to a place of personal assurance, never feeling vulnerable or needing to rely on an unsaved person being emotionally vulnerable or traumatized before feeling secure enough to witness to them. The power and effectiveness of this approach to witnessing will free any believer to witness to and win all kinds of people, regardless of an unsaved person's emotional state.

## IS EMOTIONAL/OVER THE TOP WITNESSING THE ANSWER TO SUCCESSFUL WITNESSING?

Some believers may limit witnessing to self-focused, emotional testimony along the lines of *I just want to show people how much I love Jesus* or *Jesus means everything to me!* Sharing your personal emotion of love, joy, gratitude, and enthusiasm over your life in Christ does have its place, but it is important to be equipped to balance your emotional expression of zeal for Christ with an effective plan to bring salvation closure. An overzealous testimony has the potential to turn off unbelievers that do not understand the reason for all the excitement.

Of course, believers should never let personal frustration spew out at an unbeliever under the pretense of witnessing to them. Everyone has emotions and it is not too difficult to read other people's emotional state. To express too much emotion in a witnessing exchange, whether negative or positive, has the potential to give the impression that the believer is merely a religious radical. A large segment of the unsaved world wants to identify believers as religious fanatics or apply negative political labels when referring to Christians. The love and joy of being in Jesus is a wonderful thing to express. That special love and joy is best expressed in the sensitive manner and way that an unbeliever can be sensitively worked with in the midst of a witness exchange. It is one thing to use over the top expressions of love and joy and another for an unbeliever to feel that love and joy. Believers must always be wise in witnessing and winning souls, and being equipped with your new plan you will now always make the right witnessing decisions.

## ARE UNTRAINED NEW BELIEVERS
## THE ANSWER TO SUCCESSFUL WITNESSING?

Many times new and excited believers are encouraged to go witness to unbelievers without receiving any training in how to lead
a person to Christ. I have heard it said more than once that new
believers make the best soulwinners. This is because they are on an
"emotional energy ride." Newly won and excited about the peace
and joy they have found in Christ, many new and untrained believers are encouraged to witness to their friends and to win souls. The
danger for new believers is that they are being sent into challenging
situations where rejection can easily quench their enthusiasm.

Witnessing and winning souls involves spiritual warfare. Without proper equipping, witnessing can be the most scary and intimidating event believers can face. Granted, that when first saved,
new believers are the most excited. This high emotional state
needs to be guarded and nurtured, not used for evangelistic can-
non fodder. They are new and want to shout about Jesus but with
no solid training on how to interact with unbelievers, they can be
overwhelmed, chewed up, and spit out.

Burnout is not a condition that affects only unbelievers. I think
that new-believer- burnout in witnessing is a direct contributor to
the reality that close to 90 percent of believers have never won
a soul. New believers are easy to train. When new believers are
trained to use the *Witnessing Winzone* plan, they are highly effective in bringing souls to Christ. I believe they should be trained to
win souls as soon as possible in their discipling program.

## YOU ARE THE FISHERMAN AND THE BAIT

Jesus said to Peter and Andrew, "Follow Me, and I will make
you fishers of Men" (Matt. 4:19). Jesus uses this unique analogy
regarding winning souls because fishing is an enterprise that takes
thought and wisdom to be successful. Catching fish is challenging,
fun and exciting whether it you catch only one fish or haul in a big

catch. Good fishermen know a lot about the fishing. They know where the fish are, the understand the best equipment and bait to use, and the best time of day to fish. They also know what to do with the fish after they catch them.

Effective fishermen are also good hunters; they are constantly on the hunt for the next good place to fish. Jesus has called believers to be fishers of men, which includes being hunters of good opportunities to win souls. Believers should always be watchful for an opportunity to seek out an unsaved person in order to win his or her lost soul away from Satan.

This plan is great "fishing equipment" for catching souls. Pastors and evangelists cast a big net in church services and can catch many souls. Believers can now catch them one or two at a time. All it takes for a believer to become a solid, biblical fisher of men and women is to take the time to learn your new plan. The biggest catch of all is a soul won to Jesus Christ and as you implement this approach to witnessing, you can catch them one after another for the rest of your life.

**Bait your own hook**

The best bait that a believer can have is the observable testimony of a well-lived life in Christ. Believers are going to be seen and observed by their families, friends, associates in the work place and the occasional stranger. When believers have publicly declared that they are Christians, they are going to be closely observed. Their behavior will be watched like a hawk. As solid men and women of God who are friendly toward all, let people know in normal conversation that Jesus is your Savior and let your conversation have a Christian quality to it. Be bold and, at appropriate times when something good happens, feel free to say, *Praise the Lord* or *That was the Lord.* Certainly be willing to say, *God bless you* to folks, and above all be willing to help and serve people. Believers should be willing to upgrade their visibility as Christians in all of their environments and not be ashamed or afraid to do so. Let the world know who you are in Christ by planting personal seeds through righteous actions, Godly praise statements, and integrity in your conversation and lifestyle. A believer's solid Christian lifestyle is effective bait. The most effective bait to hook and land an unbeliever is the blend of a solid lifestyle combined with the effective presentation of the Word of God.

> For I am not ashamed of the gospel of Christ, for it is the power of God to salvation for everyone who believes, for the Jew first and also for the Greek.
>
> —ROMANS 1:16

For believers to be consistently successful in witnessing and winning souls, believers need a prepared soulwinning plan, which will give them personal freedom as well as assurance and confidence as they lead unbelievers to Christ. When a witnessing believer is fully confident and assured, the unsaved will also be released to become fully assured and confident in them. Any doubt about whether you know what you are talking about is removed as the unbeliever is strategically led through the soulwinning process. Because a believer is prepared with this soulwinning plan, the unbeliever will recognize that the witnessing believer knows what he or she is talking about. Witnessing and winning souls is sort of like being in the marketplace. Would you purchase anything from anyone who does not sound like they know what they are talking about? Unbelievers are no different.

## READY FOR THE
## PERSONAL EVANGELISM ARENA

All any believer must do to become successful in soulwinning is learn to master the *Witnessing Winzone* plan for their own use. Believers must be willing to take a step of faith in soulwinning and get equipped for the arena of the unsaved world and go for it! Some believers will offer encouragement and some discouragement. Believers must choose wisely whom they will allow to influence their lives in personal evangelism. Consider the following words of wisdom:

It's not the critic who counts; not the man who points out how the strong man stumbled, or where the doer of deeds could have done better. The credit belongs to the man who is actually in the arena, in action, whose face is marred by dust and sweat and blood, who errs and comes short again and again, but who spends himself in a worthy cause, who knows the triumph of high achievement, but who if he fails, at least fails while daring greatly.[4]

—THEODORE ROOSEVELT

## THERE IS NOT "ONE WAY" TO WIN SOULS

In spite of the fact that, from my experience and the experience of many others, I know that the *Witnessing Winzone* soulwinning plan is a powerful tool for winning souls, I am aware that it is not the only way to bring people to Christ. No matter what anyone says, there is not just one specific method or approach to winning souls. The only way the phrase "one way" can relate to soulwinning is in regards to the biblical requirements for a person to be saved. According the scriptures, that one way is by responding to and accepting Jesus Christ as Savior.

This plan will equip any believer with a deep and powerful foundation to win souls in any witnessing scenario. Once learned, this soulwinning plan gives an unlimited flexibility to adapt and adjust in witnessing exchanges. It gives believers the ability to introduce the salvation gospel when the preceding conversation had nothing to do with the Bible or the things of God. In these last days believers need to be equipped and prepared for any witnessing situation that arises, and this plan provides that total preparation. The apostle Peter declared of Christ:

Nor is there salvation in any other, for there is no other name under heaven given among men by which we must be saved.

—ACTS 4:12

127

Jesus said to him, "I am the way, the truth, and the life. No one comes to the Father except through Me."

—JOHN 14:6

# A POSTMODERN CULTURE
# NEEDS TO HEAR THE WORD OF GOD

*Postmodern era* is a term philosophers use to describe the thinking processes of today, the beginning of the twenty-first century. Postmodern thought is a reaction to what was known as Modernism. Prior to the Modern Era, before the Age of Enlightenment, much of European and American thought and philosophy was Christ centered and focused on God. Architecture, literature, music, poetry, and education were God honoring. As Modernism came, man and his self-centered ability to reason were pushing out God.

Modernism began in the 1600s. It started with the Age of Enlightenment. Mankind had entered into a time of discovery and invention. In Modern thought all truth must be empirical and verifiable. Man began to think that man himself could reason, answer, and solve all problems. Human reason was the main idea in Modernism. Man can know and discover truth through his capacity to reason. In Modernism man himself could solve the future for the world and all humanity.

The collapse of Modernism began with the coming of Marxist Communism, WWI (the war to end all wars), the Great Depression, and WWII. The age of the atomic bomb, the rebellious "sixties" with the tragedy of the Vietnam War caused Postmodernism to explode as a new era. The capacity for man to reason and solve his own problems had failed. No specific truth came from his ability to reason. Their truth became the truth of relativity—interpreted truth in the moment. Many now believe that there is no absolute truth and everything is subjective. Since there is no absolute truth, why pursue the discovery of truth?

Postmodernism is a move beyond what Modernism thought about truth. Postmodern truth is a developed truth to fit the momentary situation. A Postmodern mindset might be, "I will do as I please because everything is relative to what I like. You live your life, I'll live mine! What is right for you is not right for me." Postmodern thinking is lost thinking. There is one truth and that truth is the person of Jesus Christ. Modernist and Postmodernist thinkers today are open to the salvation gospel of Jesus Christ. They just don't know it, because no one has presented the gospel of Jesus Christ to them in a way that they can hear it the right way.

Not all unbelievers today are hardcore secular Postmodernists. Many unbelievers living in this confused era are merely confused about what they really believe in a philosophical sense. They are caught up to a large degree with the idea of "relativism." Since there is not truth, everything is relative. How to respond to life challenges is relative to situations, emotions, or political attitudes of the day. Political correctness as a philosophy is attempting to force itself into the void left by relative thought. Some unbelievers claim that they are atheists because they cannot articulate what they believe and do not know what else to say.

As large as the challenges seem to appear, this Postmodern era offers the greatest opportunity of history to win souls in personal evangelism. Unbelievers are confused, unsettled in their thinking as a result of a failed relative values thought process. They do not know the truth and are searching and willing to listen, if handled correctly. Old witnessing paradigms of assuming that a believer's role-model personality and social ability to develop relationships is all that is needed to win souls needs to be upgraded. Believers need to create a balance in their personal evangelism with this powerful soulwinning plan. They need to be role models and initiate relationships when possible, but must be equipped to lead unbelievers to their decisions for Christ. Unequipped believers can be working on one relationship and miss winning a hundred others. Opportunities to win someone to Christ come and go, and believers must be equipped to act and win souls in a moment's notice.

Successful soulwinning in the Postmodern era requires a clear

understanding and presentation of the Word of God in witnessing. Unbelievers today need biblical answers that are clear and
understandable. They will respond if they hear the truth that is
clearly presented from the Word of God. Unbelievers in this era
do not know who or what to believe. It is up to believers to present
the salvation gospel in a way that it can penetrate the souls of the
lost and draw them to Jesus Christ as Lord and Savior. Unbelievers today function on a bottom-line mentality. They want information and answers that are clear and prescise. This is not new!
Unbelievers have always needed to hear a clear presentation of the
Word of God, but never more than they need it today. As believers
learn and use the *Witnessing Winzone* soulwinning plan they will
find the answer to every witnessing challenge in this Postmodern
era. Jesus said:

> I am the way, the truth, and the life. No one come to the
> Father except through Me.
>
> —JOHN 14:6

## WE MUST HURRY TO
## WIN THE YOUTH OF THE WORLD

The race for the souls of the youth of America and the world is
intense. In the era that we exist in today, the youth of the world
are being seduced and entrapped in immorality, drugs, violence,
pornography, the occult and false religions as never before. The
largest category of salvations historically has been in the age group
of 12 to 18. Historically, approximately 80 percent of all salvations
take place before the age of 18. According to the Southern Baptist
Convention these statistics are falling fast. We must rush to the
youth of America and around the world and win them to Christ,
then equip them to spread the gospel of Jesus Christ and win others
of their generation to Him. Young people are easy to win to Christ.
Once equipped with this soulwinning plan, it is just a matter of
encountering them. Unfortunately the large numbers of salva-

tions in the historically established age ranges are not taking place as they once were. When men and women reach age twenty-two and above, the numbers of salvations, percentage-wise, decrease substantially. As adults move into their thirties, forties, fifties and beyond, there are no real solid salvation statistics anywhere.

# 8

# Many Mission Fields

## BE READY ANYWHERE, ANYTIME

TRADITIONALLY WHENEVER MISSION FIELDS ARE discussed, they are generally thought of to be in another part of the world. In America, they are thought to be the far away areas of the Far East, South America, Africa, etc. From the perspective of some parts of the world, America is a mission field! Most "mission field conversations," excluding the foreign mission field, occur in the context of family, friends, work associates, visitors to your church and the occasional stranger. In this sense, a mission field can be a place of work, neighborhood, playground, gym, etc. The mission fields that believers find themselves in are really mixes of all of these circumstances. In short, the mission field where you can serve is wherever you happen to be at the moment. Jesus and the Holy Spirit have already prepared untold numbers of unsaved people to be won to Jesus as Savior wherever they are found.

The following is an overview of several common types of "mission fields" where individual believers live and work:

- *Family*: Members of the immediate family and extended family who are unsaved. Many times the people in this mission field can be quite challenging, but there is always

132

a way to approach them. The best way is to evaluate family relationships with unsaved family members and, if necessary, "start over" with them. Starting over means there may need to be some fence-mending and apologizing for any arguments you may have been involved with. Starting over also requires a season without witnessing during which you can be praying for a new opportunity to start over. It is a humbling approach to regain any lost credibility in the family, but a fresh start can be created. Pray for the right time to witness again and be equipped to introduce the family member to Jesus Christ by using the *Witnessing Winzone* soulwinning plan.

- *Friends and Work Associates*: They can be almost as challenging as family. People who are in close, constant proximity can always be challenging. It is wise to interact daily with unbelievers with a humble assurance, and they will understand you are after their best interest. Some of these relationships will need a new beginning, so be prepared to humble yourself and pray for fresh opportunities to start over and witness anew.

- *Church*: The church is a somewhat hidden mission field for believers because in many cases the mission field has come to the church. As believers attend churches around the world many are unaware that seeking unbelievers are in their midst. Oftentimes, many believers overlook these same seeking unbelievers because there is the unspoken assumption that *Pastor* will deal with them. And many believers are in church to have their own needs met. The Southern Baptist Convention believes that approximately 50 percent of church visitors are unsaved. Much of the evangelism promotion of today is for members to encourage the unsaved to come to church to hear the message. Members are going out into their immediate mission fields and inviting people to their church, creating a mission field within the Church itself.

- *Occasional Stranger*: Remember when Jesus met the woman at the well and when Philip approached the eunuch? When you know how to win souls, a day will come when you will find yourself in any one of a thousand places and the Lord will put it on your heart to witness to a stranger. The first time you may be nervous. What is amazing is that because you have learned this soulwinning plan you will immediately discover that everything you learned in this book is true. You will easily win them to Christ, and your life and theirs will be changed forever.

Unless God calls you to some far away land, there is a ready mission field where every believer lives, works and plays. It is wise for believers to be aware of their individual circumstances and environments. Every environment that believers exist in is a mission field. The body of Christ must never forget that the greatest mission fields are wherever they happen to be. It is the men, women, boys, girls, Jews and gentiles alike, who are the mission, in the places where they live, work, travel and interact every day of the week.

## FAMILY CHALLENGES

The most challenging people to win to Christ are members of a believer's family. Family members will generally be more vocal about you and what you have done in your life than casual friends. They will not hesitate to express what they think about your life in Christ. They have known you all of your life and have an established perspective of who you are. I know that there are instances when believers end up not speaking with some family members. There could have been arguments and even shouting matches. Are you someone who is frustrated with a family member? Is there a history of argument and tension? Something to consider is the following and you are going to have to humble yourself to do it. These are suggestions to consider and are some common sense approaches.

- First, pray and go to the family member and be willing to apologize for any problems that you may have created or perceived to have created. Ultimately, it doesn't matter if it is your fault or not. What is important is to create a fresh start in the relationship. Help them to experience the love of Jesus in you instead of just the words about Jesus that come out of you.

- Second, back off from any over-aggressive witnessing and give them some breathing room. Begin to pray for that unsaved loved one and pray for the Lord to open the right time for you to reintroduce a loving witness exchange. All of a sudden you may find the right opportunity to say, "I talk to a lot of people about Jesus Christ, salvation and eternal life"

- Third, if they are in your home or community, look for ways to reach out and serve them when you can. Be willing to humble yourself and lay a bruised ego down. It may take a while for them to become ready to receive your new witness.

- Fourth, one of the most effective tools to win family members is the telephone. Many families are separated by distance and see one another on special occasions only. This soulwinning plan is very effective on the telephone.

If a family member has been distant or unfriendly, believers must be willing to forgive and forget about how the other family member behaved. Take a step of faith and forgive them; loose any anger toward them and make winning them to Christ a goal. Romans 12:20 says:

Therefore, if your enemy is hungry, feed him; If he is thirsty, give him a drink; for in so doing you will heap coals of fire on his head.

Let the Lord do the convicting. Condemnation never works; it only serves to enlarge separation between people. Let the Holy Spirit use your loving-kindness to convict and break their hardened heart and fully trust the Holy Spirit to move upon them; then all of a sudden one day you will find yourself having a sensitive and general witnessing conversation. In that conversation you will know that the time is right and you will hear yourself begin to say, "I talk to a lot of people about Jesus Christ, salvation and eternal life. Do you mind if I ask you a question without being too personal?" The Bible says in 2 Timothy 4:2:

> Preach the Word! Be ready in season and out of season. Convince, rebuke, exhort, with all longsuffering and teaching.

This scripture is encouraging the body of Christ to be equipped and prepared to instantly present the gospel, no matter what the circumstances. Being equipped with your new plan will give you the ability to respond immediately at every opportunity.

## HIS JEWISH BROTHER CAME TO CHRIST

A young man, whom I will call Ralph, was a believer with a Jewish heritage. He could never find a way to talk to his brother about receiving Jesus as his Savior. He lived in constant frustration because he wanted his brother to come to the Lord, but he could not figure out how to do it. After learning to use the *Witnessing Winzone* approach to winning souls, the following week he led his brother to the Messiah.

## REASONS MANY DON'T WITNESS

Out of frustration, most believers have given up hope of actually leading a lost soul to salvation. They have mentally and emotionally turned the task of winning souls over to the paid professionals. They believe that all evangelism efforts should be made by pastors, evangelists and church staff or to those that they assume have an exclusive gifting to win souls. Many in the body of Christ feel challenged by a combination of issues that individually all combine to paralyze them, keeping them from witnessing at a basic level. These obstacles are easy to understand and just as easy to overcome:

1. Some feel that witnessing is not their calling. Perhaps they have developed a deep personal attitude that God will use others and so it is just not necessary for them to witness. Some think, *I just don't have enough faith to witness*. Others think *witnessing is not my gift*.

2. Some feel they don't have enough Bible knowledge. They think, Other people are more trained and equipped than I. God knows who they are and will use them; therefore I do not need to be involved.

3. Some feel they don't know how to introduce the gospel message graciously. Some think, I get excited too easily and just get into fusses and fights. Some feel others have a better temperament for this sort of thing and think, I just don't have enough patience with those unsaved people. Others are better than I; let them do it or I cannot deal with controversy.

4. Some feel they should just be a silent witness and let their good lifestyle speak for them. The thought is, People who really know me know that I love Jesus and anyone who is interested can see that I live a good life. I don't need to talk about it. I'm uncomfortable talking about God and Jesus.

5. Some feel the unsaved have too much Bible crammed upon them and they do not want to be one of those who oppress or bother the lost. They don't want people to think that they are just another one of those Bible thumpers. They have an attitude that says unsaved people will know plenty if they will go to church. It is their

business. I don't want to stir things up. I definitely do not want to go looking for trouble. People are turned off if too many Christians "bug" them about Jesus.

6. Some believers are trapped in different aspects of fear, such as:

*The fear of rejection.* They fear rejection because they are convinced that they will only hear No and have almost a zero opportunity of actually winning a lost soul to Christ. A Christian may have witnessed at one time or another but because of inadequate preparation they had no success in actually leading someone to Christ and it was easier to just give up.

*The fear of the unknown.* Fear of the unknown is a very real issue because if Christians are not properly trained they have no idea what to expect. Going into the unknown can be a scary proposition because in that unknown is the possibility of a negative encounter that is not appealing to anyone.

*The fear of failure.* The fear of failure is a subtle problem in the Church. Almost all of the evangelical church one way or another is promoting the church to win the lost and there is a tremendous amount of pressure to be a person who wins souls. Too many in the body of Christ feel much safer doing nothing since, if there is no attempt, there is no failure.

7. Some believers live in a state of apathy. At some point the issues of life just crowd out the personal desire to become outwardly evangelical and actively witness. Men and women in the body of Christ engage all sorts of people about all kinds of issues on a daily basis. The concept of witnessing feels like it is just too much and Christians slide into a kind of mental indifference.

8. The worldly philosophy of live and let live weaves itself into the mentality of some believers. Negative ideas such as, people should mind their own business and I can't

live other people's lives for them have convinced many believers to do nothing.

With the *Witnessing Winzone* soulwinning plan believers can instantly start winning souls and completely overcome any challenging thoughts and ideas in the mind of unbelievers. As soon as believers are equipped with this plan any negative thoughts that they might have had about witnessing and winning souls are forgotten and will never return.

## SHE SAID, "BUT I DON'T TALK TO PEOPLE!"

A young lady attended one of my soulwinning seminars and told me that she had a difficult time talking to people. She said that she was generally afraid of witnessing to people. She told me that one afternoon she and an unsaved friend were sitting in her car and she literally read the *Witnessing Winzone* sequence to her friend and led her friend to the Lord. She was thrilled and amazed that the friend followed along perfectly as she read to her. It is not designed to be read to people, but in her first steps in learning to win souls, it worked!

9

# Relational, Flexible, and Equipped

## PREPAREDNESS OPENS THE DOOR TO FLEXIBILITY

IN 1 CORINTHIANS 9:19–22 PAUL states:

> For though I am free from all men, I have made myself a
> servant to all, that I might win the more; and to the Jews
> I became as a Jew, that I might win Jews; to those who are
> under the law, as under the law, that I might win those who
> are under the law; to those who are without law, as with-
> out law (not being without law toward God, but under law
> toward Christ), that I might win those who are without law;
> to the weak I became as weak, that I might win the weak. I
> have become all things to all men, that I might by all means
> save some.

Paul is expressing a profound willingness to be flexible and relational in his approach to personal evangelism in order to win more
souls. He is writing specifically about soulwinning evangelism.
And he is declaring his willingness to approach people according
to their background and circumstances as he presents Christ to
them. Ultimately, relationships that are ongoing have flexibility
built into them. Much has been written to encourage believers
to evangelize through developing relationships. Many times the

depth of a relationship will determine the effectiveness of encouraging discipleship.

Having a willingness to develop relationships in order to win souls is a worthy goal. However, some believers may feel that in order to win someone to Christ they must make an unbeliever their new best friend. That is simply not true. Relationships alone are not the key to winning souls. As we have discussed, learning how to win souls is the key to winning souls. Believers who work to develop relationships in order to witness by selling themselves, without knowing how to win souls, can be like putting the cart before the horse. That is partially why an estimated 90 percent of the body of Christ have never won a soul to Christ.

Believers are always going to develop relationships, but what is vital is to know how to actually win people to Christ. Believers must have a balanced soulwinning perspective in how they view potential relationships with the unsaved. Some relationships will be deeper and more significant than others. It is important for believers to be equipped to win any unbeliever no matter what the depth of their relationship—long-term, short-term, or temporary. Clever and novel approaches to outreach come and go, but a trained soulwinner will continually win souls.

## IS YOUR IDENTITY
## BASED ON KNOWLEDGE OR CARING?

Unbelievers want to sense how much you care more than how much you know. There is always a sensitive balance in having a relationship with an unsaved person. Believers must meet the unsaved where they are and treat them with love and respect. Many times the unsaved want to experience or sense how much a believer cares about them, more than how much information the believer knows. Believers can show the love of Jesus by being available to help, serve and meet them at their points of need.

Believers should be sensitive and willing to help people at any point of need, immediate problem or crisis. Unbelievers' needs, challenges and conflicts are open doors for believers to be a friend and to win them to Jesus. Be quick and willing to help in simple ways. Don't try to pretend to be anything that you are not; just be yourself. After becoming soulwinners, believers will begin to see small acts of kindness as open doors of opportunity. What is key in these doors of opportunity is that a believer must know what to say when they walk through them. Be helpful and at the same time aim for a soulwinning result.

## SHE NEVER STOPS WINNING SOULS

At one of my earlier soulwinning seminars, a young lady who was a single mom was excited about learning how to win souls. She had no car and used public transportation through the bus system to go to her domestic housekeeping jobs. She rides the bus and wins the people that sit next to her. She has done so countless numbers of times. She sits next to people, visits with them, introduces this same soulwinning plan and wins many to Jesus as Savior on the bus and then invites them to church. She has been consistently winning souls for many years using the same plan you are learning

## ASSERT SENSITIVE AUTHORITY

As ambassadors for Christ, believers are His representation and His representatives. Just as Adam and Eve were created in the image of God representing Him, believers are to live lives representing Jesus Christ, the Son. In doing so, they explain the good news of salvation to a lost and dying world as ambassadors for Jesus Christ. Ambassadors always have credentials to give them authority to speak on behalf of whomever they represent. The church has full authority from biblical credentials to speak on behalf of Jesus Christ. The apostle Paul declares in 2 Corinthians 5:20 declares: "Now then we are Ambassadors for Christ." When believers witness they need to know they can do so with authority. The safest and strongest way to deal with non-believers is from a position of loving and tactful control of the conversation.

Either a believer is going to control the witnessing exchange or an unbeliever is going to control the witnessing exchange. Someone is going to be in control of the conversation. It needs to be the witnessing believer. It is imperative that believers exercise their godly authority at all times and be willing to gently guide the witness exchange to where it needs to go. It is important in personal evangelism to understand that believers have authority and that they should take and maintain gentle control of a witnessing exchange. It is critical for believers to realize that they not only have godly authority according to the scriptures, they must assert that authority and assume control of witnessing exchanges.

> Behold, I send you out as sheep in the midst of wolves. Therefore be wise as serpents and harmless as doves.
>
> —MATTHEW 10:16

## MOVE FAST—BATTLES ARE WON OR LOST IN MINUTES

The apostle Paul exhorted Timothy, "Preach the word! Be ready in season and out of season. Convince, rebuke, exhort with all long-suffering and teaching" (2 Tim. 4:2). Believers must be ready and willing to act immediately in situations, when witnessing circumstances are as we like them and even when they aren't. This is important because many believers will need to come to grips with the reality that witnessing is not just about their personal comfort zone. Believers are in spiritual warfare, contending for lost souls. Believers must be willing to be assertive in order to win these spiritual battles. To be assertive in this context means to be willing to move briskly when appropriate and follow through to closure. That is one of the strengths of the *Witnessing Winzone* plan, that it can be presented in a very short time.

## ALL AGES, RACES, AND CULTURES

This soulwinning plan is powerful and effective no matter what the age of the person to whom you are witnessing. It is amazing that as people get older and come closer to a time when they are going to die, they seem to be more resistant to the claims of Christ. That is simply a general observation of people in their forties, fifties, sixties and above. The older unbelievers get, the more they seem to negotiate life by developing different mental survival systems. Casual witnessing does not seem to be effective with older people, but when the *Witnessing Winzone* plan is successfully presented, it dramatically breaks through any age barrier.

## HOW A VERY SENIOR CITIZEN CAME TO CHRIST

I once went on a sales appointment and a very senior man answered the door. It was a warm summer day. He did not have a shirt on; suspenders held up his trousers. He had a long white beard and looked like he was a hundred years old if he was a day. He was standing behind a screen door sort of bracing himself against the doorframe. I immediately knew that the only reason I was there was to lead him to the Lord. After polite but brief conversation, I introduced this soulwinning plan, and through our screen door conversation, I can still see his face and hear his words. I asked him the key questions and at the end when I presented Romans 10:9 he suddenly asked, *What must I do to be saved?* I couldn't believe my ears! He was then easy to lead in a prayer to receive Jesus Christ as Savior. Statistics do not exist to tell how many people age 50–60 and above receive Christ. When people get to be 35 and 40 years of age and older, there are few statistics on the number of conversions among their age group. Believers, you never know whom you are going to encounter. It does not matter if they are young or old, they are all easily won to Christ when you are equipped to present the gospel in a clear and powerful way.

## RACIALLY AND CULTURALLY SENSITIVE

Our approach to witnessing must be racially and culturally sensitive to confidently win the souls of those who are of another race and culture. In times of so much tension from racial and cultural divisions, the salvation gospel of Jesus Christ is the great equalizer. I have witnessed to and won men, women, boys, and girls to Christ from every race using this approach. The message of the cross applies to all of humanity. In presenting Christ, the focus in upon Him. All of humanity is in the same boat, so to speak. We all need Him together, regardless of our background, race or culture. The accurate presentation of Jesus Christ as Savior through the *Witnessing Winzone* plan will break through all social, gender, racial, cultural and socio-economic challenges in sharing the gospel. In Galatians 3:26–29 we read:

> For you are all sons of God through faith in Christ Jesus. For as many of you as were baptized into Christ have put on Christ. There is neither Jew nor Greek, there is neither slave nor free, there is neither male nor female; for you are all one in Christ Jesus.

## HE DIED BEFORE DAWN

One Sunday a woman from our congregation approached me and asked if I would go to a hospital and pray for a young man dying of AIDS. She had worked with him and wanted me to win him to Christ. I said *yes* and promised that I would go to the hospital. I arrived at the hospital room, where I was expected and met the dying young man's mother. I told her specifically why I was there. We both knew his death was imminent. She was a believer and wanted her son to be saved. She stated that his family had been praying for him. Surprisingly, she was hesitant at first about my entering the room because her son's homosexual partner and other homosexual friends were also in the room. She was intimidated and unsure whether she should get permission from the son's homosexual partner for me to talk to her son. I told her as lovingly as I could, "I am not here to deal with any politically correct gay agenda. This is your son and I am not interested in the other relationship. He is about to die. If you want to see your son saved, I am here to lead him to the Lord. Forget the homosexual partner and let's go directly to your son's bedside." She agreed and we entered the room.

At his bed I openly confirmed with him that he knew that he was about to die at any moment. I instructed his mother to take his hand. I told him what I was going to do and said that when He was accepting Jesus as Savior to squeeze her hand; he could barely whisper. I presented the *Witnessing Winzone* approach to salvation in a loud enough voice so everyone in the room could hear; I was very direct in speaking to the dying young man. He squeezed his mother's hand as I led him to Christ. She cried for joy. The homosexual partner and friends were upset—they said I was insensitive. The young man died before dawn.

Sometimes you are called upon to assert Godly authority and take control of more than one situation at a time. What was important was that this dying young man had the opportunity to clearly hear the Word of God; he responded and his sins were forgiven. Was he discipled? No. He was like the thief on the cross. In the last moments of his young life, he prayed for Jesus to be his Savior. If believers are equipped to win souls they can be used in some very last minute salvation experiences. These kinds of situations are not the norm, but they do happen. Be prepared in case they do and remember the mercy of God shown to the thief on the cross:

> Then one of the criminals who were hanged blasphemed Him, saying, "If You are the Christ, save Yourself and us."
>
> But the other, answering, rebuked him, saying, "Do you not even fear God, seeing you are under the same condemnation? And we indeed justly, for we receive the due reward of our deeds; but this Man has done nothing wrong." Then he

said to Jesus, "Lord, remember me when You come into Your kingdom."

And Jesus said to him, "Assuredly, I say to you, today you will be with Me in Paradise."

—LUKE 23:39–43

## YOU MAKE THE LIFE AND DEATH DIFFERENCE

For some unsaved, you may be the last hope for them to find eternal life. Not one person knows the time or date of their coming death. Death is certainly coming for us all and like a heroic firefighter you can possibly be used in the last minute to pull someone out of impending and certain eternal disaster. The Bible says in Jude 22,

> And on some having compassion, making a distinction; but others save with fear, pulling them out of the fire, hating even the garment defiled by the flesh.

## SOULWINNING, WITNESS, AND SHARING

After you start using your new soulwinning plan, you will realize firsthand that there is a dramatic difference between it and other methods of soulwinning, witnessing, sharing, sharing personal testimony, or sharing your faith. The body of Christ is generally familiar with these evangelistic terms and has a sense of what they mean when they hear other believers use them. It is generally assumed that all believers understand the differences in these terms. The uphill battle is not only to understand what all these terms mean but be able to apply them on a practical level. The following is a brief overview of these terms. Upon mastering your new plan, you will experience a fresh perspective on evangelism language and the application of the language as never before.

The term soulwinning could have come from Paul or it could also have come from Proverbs 11:30b, *And he who wins souls is wise.*

Paul states that he, above all things, wants to participate in winning. So just what is it he wants to win? Arguments? Ideas? Political stands? Paul is writing about winning souls to Jesus Christ. Paul's number one priority is winning souls, and he is willing to humble himself and adapt to personalities and lifestyles as a strategy to get close enough to people to win them to Christ.

> For though I am free from all men, I have made myself a servant to all, that I might win the more.
>
> — 1 CORINTHIANS 9:19

The following are some basic definitions of familiar terms used in the arena of winning souls to Christ:

1. *Soulwinning* is the process of winning a soul away from the kingdom of Satan into the kingdom of God. This process involves a skill that can easily be mastered. *Webster's Dictionary* defines *skill* as "practical ability and dexterity."[1] Soulwinning is a learnable skill because it can be taught. The skill for winning souls is developed by using the various essential components of this soulwinning plan, which are blended in a way that leads to a soulwinning conclusion. It combines your efforts as a Christian with a goal, the Holy Spirit, and the Word of God all in the name of Jesus Christ. The only prerequisite to learn how to win souls with the *Witnessing Winzone* plan is the desire to win souls. Learning to win souls does not require a particular spiritual gifting, academic achievement or any specific personality type.

2. The term *witnessing* as a process of communication is used by Jesus in His instructions to His disciples: "And you shall be witnesses to Me in Jerusalem, and in all Judea and Samaria, and to the end of the earth" (Acts 1:8). According to *The New Webster's Dictionary*, to be a witness involves: "testimony; one who, or that which, furnishes evidence or proof; one who has seen or has knowledge of incidents; one who attests another person's signature to a document; to be witness of or to; to give

evidence; to testify."[2] Witnessing is a believer's communication to an unbeliever about his experience in Christ and how an unbeliever can also receive Christ. In Jesus' reference to believers as being His witnesses, He is talking about being empowered by the Holy Spirit to witness on His behalf. Anytime believers talk about their personal experience and knowledge of Jesus Christ, that is considered witnessing.

3. *Sharing* is general conversation about religious faith and one's own experience in Christ. Sharing is basically a dialogue between the believer and an unbeliever, talking about a variety of issues, in which the believer tries to keep the conversation centered on the gospel of Jesus. Sharing your faith can be more of a monologue when personal testimony is being presented. Often the process of witnessing is described by using the term *sharing*. The concept of sharing has a tenderness attached to it, a gentleness of tone, and is connected to the process of witnessing about very personal issues. When believers talk about the blessings of God with each other, that is also considered sharing.

## COMBINATION OF TESTIMONY AND OPENNESS

Witnessing as we consider it today is generally made up of personal testimony, which for the most part is a believer's conversation about his or her own personal journey in Christ. It may or may not include some information about a believer's life before coming to Christ. It could also include a broad, sweeping statement of personal life conditions surrounding a decision for coming to Christ. This will depend on how much or how little a believer feels comfortable sharing about themselves. Witnessing can include talking about general knowledge of the Bible and how those biblical points relate to the individual or to the issues of the person or persons being witnessed to.

Witnessing can flow back and forth on a variety of issues. The value of this soulwinning plan is that it gives a believer a place to conclude, giving the witnessing exchange the structure and control that it needs to have. Witnessing can have a wandering around quality to it. If believers know how they are going to conclude, the wandering around quality doesn't matter. What is important is that the witnessing believer knows where they eventually want to lead an unbeliever and how to get there.

## TELEPHONES ARE GREAT
## SOULWINNING TOOLS—PHONE HOME

As I mentioned earlier, one of the most effective tools in winning souls can be your telephone. I have led several people to the Lord over the telephone. If you have relatives and friends who live in other cities, towns or states, the telephone can be just as effective as your sitting next to them in their living room. Believers can win souls long-distance by introducing unbelievers to the *Witnessing Winzone* plan while on the telephone. A telephone conversation can be just as intimate as talking with someone in person and many times it can feel less threatening. Winning souls on the telephone is quite easy. All believers have long-distance relatives and former friends who would love to hear from you. At the appropriate time in your phone conversation you can gently start with, "You know, _____, I talk to a lot of people about Jesus Christ, salvation, and eternal life...."

**Won on the telephone**

One morning the Lord awakened me around 4:30 a.m., California time. It was as if He was shouting a woman's name whom I knew from my youth in Lockhart, Texas. Her name was swirling around my head like a swarm of bees. She was a past friend of my mother's and I felt strongly impressed to call and witness to her. I did call and we had a wonderful reunion conversation; then I introduced the soulwinning plan. When I introduced the eternal danger question, *When you die and it is time for you to go to heaven and Jesus Christ asks you, why should I let you into heaven and give you eternal life? What would you say to Jesus?* she immediately answered, "Brent, I don't know and I have cancer. When I got married my uncle told me to settle down and get into church, so I did, but I don't know." I then proceeded to lead her to her decision to receive Jesus Christ as her Savior. She died within months.

I have led others to the Lord over the telephone. It is non-threatening and, as I have said, there can be a conversation that is just as intimate as if you were speaking face to face. If you have distant family members or friends who are unsaved, the telephone is a great way to reach out and win them.

## PEOPLE IN STRESS AND CATASTROPHE

When dealing with an unsaved person who is facing a painful problem, always show the love of Jesus in your tender handling of his or her concern. As you love them and they sense your caring, there will be an opportunity to gently lead them to Jesus. As you sense the leading of the Holy Spirit tell them, *"God loves you and has an answer for your needs. I want to pray with you for God to bless you and touch your life, but before I do that, may I ask you a question without being too personal?"* Then continue to present the plan of salvation.

Believers must always be sensitive to what is going on with a person. Yet, even in a sensitive moment, believers must be willing to seize the moment to win the hurting soul. When believers are equipped and assured to do so, it is an uncomplicated soulwinning process. In these difficult situations, continue to lead them to Christ when you think it is appropriate.

Believers should always use their own judgment in any encounter with an unsaved person. An alternative to the above scenario is to pray for their specific need and then at the conclusion of that prayer say to them, "God bless you_____(name)." After a short pause, say, "You know, I talk to a lot of people about Jesus Christ, salvation and eternal life . . . ." Then continue!

## Win God's Chosen People

If you are witnessing to a Jewish person, when you introduce the *Witnessing Winzone* plan there is just one more simple statement to include. As you are explaining Rom 3:23, simply include this wording:

> And so, _____ (name), as a result of that original sin in the Garden of Eden, we are all born spiritually separated from God. The Bible is the story of God creating mankind, man falling into sin, and God trying to reconcile all of humanity back unto Him. He started with His covenant with Abraham, and then Moses brought the Law and the sacrificial system for sin. Ultimately Jesus came to be the sacrificial Lamb for the sins of the world... (and then continue on).

This is a simple story that ties Jewish history into our message. What is significant is that we are acknowledging their Jewish history. Many Jews are not necessarily religious, they are cultural and secular Jews who have a limited knowledge of Scripture. The Orthodox Jews are the exception. Much of the Jewish community is considered either Conservative or Reform, and receive most of their teaching from the Talmud and not directly out of Scripture.

The Jewish people on a broad scale are deeply challenged about coming to Jesus as Savior. They are raised from birth to deny Him. If they accept Christ, their families may completely disown and/or shun them. It is a great step of faith for them to come to Christ. It is far easier for the Gentile community to come to Christ, but people of Jewish heritage will absolutely respond to the salvation gospel of Jesus Christ as presented through this plan.

## Witnessing to a Buddhist
## or Any in an Anti-Christ Religion

This is a reference that illustrates and discusses witnessing to anyone who identifies with a religion that is not Christian. Witnessing to a Buddhist is really like witnessing to anyone else. Trust the Word of God as you present the plan of salvation. Buddhists do not believe in God as Christians understand Him and do not have a concept of an absolute God. Buddhists believe that ignorance is the problem, not sin. Buddha is worshiped as an example of a saintly life. Their concept of salvation is based on reaching a mental state of nirvana, but somehow believe it is selfish to enter into a state of salvation unless all of humanity can join them. nirvana seems to be an endless mental state of transcendence to a higher level of thought, a state based upon meditation and self-denial. Buddhism teaches that there are Four Noble Truths:

- Life is basically suffering or has dissatisfaction. The origin of suffering is in craving or grasping for something.

- The stoppage of suffering is possible through the stoppage of craving.

- The way to stop craving and to not have repeated rebirth is by following Buddhist practices.

- Ultimately a Buddhist seeks to eliminate his or her self and become passive and compassionate in order to reach nirvana, the total transcendental state.

If you share with a Buddhist, be assured and aware that they have no hidden truth. They are not on some higher plane of understanding, as they may want you to believe. Buddhists are men and women who are grasping at something to hold onto in life. Buddhists have no particular insight into anything. Do not be overwhelmed or intimidated by a Buddhist or any other exotic sounding religion. If anyone identifies spiritually with a person or group other than Jesus Christ they are in great eternal danger.

## FIRST TIME FOR THEM

Always keep in mind that even though you know what you are going to say and where you want to lead them, the unsaved may not have a clue as to what is going on. What you are asking and presenting to them may be totally new to them. It is possible that they know nothing about what you are about to ask them or where you are about to lead them. Never fall into the trap of trying to second-guess what you think the unsaved are thinking. Never think that they are anticipating what you are going to ask them. When you present this soulwinning plan to an unsaved person, it will probably be the first time for them. No matter how much you know or do not know about the Bible—and it may be a lot or a little—rest assured that an unsaved person would not know what you know or understand.

# 10

# Unbelievers Might Say Anything

AS YOU KNOW, IN THE basic model of the *Witnessing Winzone* soulwinning plan, after you ask the main questions, you are waiting a response. An unsaved person may respond with any kind of statements. Keep in mind that you have asked them a question that is very difficult for them to deal with. You have caught them off guard or sort of flat footed. You have eased them into and asked them the eternal danger question, which is:

> Let me ask you this, "When you die and it's time for you to go to Heaven, and Jesus Christ asks you, 'Why should I let you into Heaven and give you eternal life?' what would you say to Jesus?"

This is a strategic question that an unsaved person will have a difficult time wrestling with. They may say anything. The following are several different responses that I have heard over the years. I have included suggestions for ways to respond to them. This is a time to be wise, sensitive, and flexible with your response to their response. It is never a good time to say to an unbeliever, *Are you nuts?* Even though you may think what they say sounds crazy, don't say it! Also maintain a clam demeanor. Don't smirk or have a "know-it-all" look on your face.

## Your Response to Their Responses

These responses are typical responses, for which I explain how to deflect their responses and not make an issue of them. *These are just possible references you can be familiar with; they are not meant to be memorized.* The goal here is to keep the unsaved person from creating a new conversation agenda, one that makes you feel you have to directly challenge their response. The idea is for you to use their response to transition to the presentation of the Word of God. That comes through their open response, which confirms that they know little about the eternal death issue. You then use your soft response to their response as the bridge to present the salvation gospel of Jesus Christ.

Remember, you may hear something shocking! Just don't act shocked because the unsaved person will read your response or reaction like a book. If you respond and behave as if whatever they say is normal, you may diffuse a potentially volatile situation. Stay calm, loving and compassionate; and they will absolutely follow you as you lead them to Jesus Christ as Savior. At all costs never make a negative facial or vocal expression to show disgust or disapproval of an unsaved person's response. Resist the temptation to express any negative form of expression that implies your own superiority about Biblical matters.

Always understand that no matter what the unsaved person says in response to your question, it is okay for them to say what they just said. You are not going to agree with them or disagree with them openly. Privately you know the truth and that is what is important. You want to lead them into the truth of Jesus Christ. Stay calm, cool and collected, and let the unsaved say what they want. Then handle their response with some variation of, *You know, that's a normal response. A lot of people feel that way. But let me share something the Bible says about that for you today. In Rom 3:23 the Bible says, "For all have sinned and . . . (Continue on)."*

## RESPONSES TO THE
## ETERNAL DANGER QUESTION

Refer again to the eternal danger question at the beginning of this chapter, and then consider the following examples of typical responses of unbelievers to that question, which you should be familiar with. It is important to create an awareness of them because you will probably hear them. Then consider the example of an appropriate response you can offer. Do not try to memorize them, just review, be aware, and be ready for them because they will come one way or another. They are all easy to deal with when you are prepared with your soulwinning plan:

- *I've tried to be a good person and live a good life.* You respond, "You know Joe, that's a pretty normal response. I think most people would like to think that they have tried to live a good life. Joe, let me share something with you that the Bible says about that for you, today. In Romans 3:23, the Bible says…"(and continue on).

- *I don't believe in Heaven or hell.* You respond, "You know Joe, that's a pretty normal response. There are a lot of people who don't believe in Heaven or hell. Joe, let me share something with you that the Bible says about that for you, today. In Romans 3:23 the Bible says…" (and continue on).

- *I don't believe in Jesus or salvation.* You respond, "You know Joe, that's a pretty normal response. There are a lot of people who don't believe in Jesus or salvation. Joe, let me share something with you that the Bible says about that for you, today. In Rom 3:23 the Bible says…"(and continue on).

- *I don't believe in the Bible.* You respond, "You know Joe, that's a normal and a very honest response. There are a lot of people who don't believe in the Bible. Joe, let me share something with you that the Bible says about that for you, today. In Romans 3:23 the Bible says..."(and continue on).

- *I believe there are many paths to God.* You respond, "You know Joe, that's a normal response, because a lot of people believe that there are many paths to God. Joe, let me share something with you that the Bible says about that for you, today. In Romans 3:23 the Bible says..."(and continue on).

- *I believe an all-knowing God would know that without having to ask me.* You respond, "You know Joe, that's a very normal and insightful answer. What is key is, He always wants to hear what we believe. Joe, let me share something with you that the Bible says about that for you, today. In Romans 3:23 the Bible says..."(and continue on).

- *I don't know that He would ask me a question like that.* You respond, "Joe, that is a normal response and an interesting observation. His words may vary slightly but He is going to ask us all to give an accounting for our lives. Joe, let me share something with you that the Bible says about that for you, today. In Romans 3:23 the Bible says..."(and continue on).

- *Because I deserve it.* You respond, "Joe, that is a pretty normal response. I think most people would like to think that they have lived a life good enough to go to Heaven. They didn't try to hurt anyone and tried to live a good life just like you. Joe, let me share something with you that the Bible says about that for you, today. In Romans 3:23 the Bible says..."(and continue on).

- *As I was growing up I attended a church.* You respond, "Joe, that's a normal response. A lot of people grew up attending church and have tried to live a good life. Joe, let me share something with you that the Bible says about that for you, today. In Romans 3:23 the Bible says..."(and continue on).

- *I'm a religious person.* You respond, "Joe, that's a normal response from people who are religious. Could you tell me what you mean by religious?" (Let them explain themselves. They could possibly be saved but do not assume that they are. No matter what they say, continue.) "That's an interesting answer. I think a lot of people want to be religious. Joe, let me share something with you that the Bible says about that for you, today. In Romans 3:23 the Bible says..."(and continue on).

- *My father was a deacon in the church.* You respond, "Joe, that's a normal response and it sounds like you come from a good family. Joe, let me share something with you that the Bible says about that for you, today. In Romans 3:23 the Bible says..." (and continue on).

- *I believe everyone goes to Heaven.* You respond, "Joe, that's a normal response. A lot of people believe everyone gets to go to Heaven, and it sounds like you are counting on it. Joe, let me share something with you that the Bible says about that for you, today. In Romans 3:23 the Bible says"... (and continue on).

- *I believe we just die and that's it.* You respond, "Joe, that's an honest answer and a normal response because a lot of people believe we just die and that is all there is. Joe, let me share something with you that the Bible says about that for you today. In Romans 3:23 the Bible says..." (and continue on).

- *I don't care if I go to Heaven or not.* You respond, "Joe, that's a normal response. I've talked to other people that felt that way. Joe, let me share something with you that the Bible says about that for you, today. In Romans 3:23 the Bible says..."(and continue on).

- *God lets anyone into Heaven who deserves it.* You respond, "Joe, that's normal response. A lot of people feel that if they deserve Heaven, they should be allowed in. Joe, let me share something with you that the Bible says about that for you, today. In Romans 3:23 the Bible says..."(and continue on).

- *We're all God's children and He won't send anyone away.* You respond, "Joe, that's a normal response. A lot of people feel the same way. Let me share with you something with you that the Bible says about that for you, today. In Romans 3:23 the Bible says..."(and continue on).

- *My karma will get me to Heaven.* You respond, "Joe, that's a normal response because a lot of people feel that they've tried to live a good life and will get to Heaven because of their good works. Let me share something with you that the Bible says about that for you today. In Romans 3:23 the Bible says..."(and continue on).

- *I believe in Buddha.* You respond, "Joe, that's a normal response. There are a lot of people who believe in Buddhism, but have questions about Heaven. Let me share something with you that the Bible says about that for you today. In Romans 3:23 the Bible says..."(and continue on).

- *I believe we are all God.* You respond, "Joe, that's a normal response. Other people believe the same thing. Let me share with you something the Bible says about that for you today. In Romans 3:23 the Bible says..."(and continue on).

- *I'll accept Jesus when I'm ready, when I think it is the right time.* You respond, "Joe, that's a normal response. A lot of people want to come to God when they think it is the right time. Unfortunately none of us know when we might die or be killed. Let me share with you something

the Bible says about that for you today. In Romans 3:23
the Bible says"... (and continue on).

- *I believe in reincarnation and so I don't worry about dying.*
  You respond, "Joe, that's a normal response. A lot of
  people believe in reincarnation. Let me share with you
  something the Bible says about that for you today. First,
  in Hebrews 9:27 the Bible says, "And as it is appointed
  for men to die once, but after this the judgment..."
  The Bible says that because in Romans 3:23 the Bible
  says..."(and continue on).

**Most responses are pushovers**

These examples of responses from unsaved people are generally
what you are going to hear. As you familiarize yourself with these
simple examples of appropriate responses to unbelievers' responses,
you will be well prepared for any answers unbelievers might give to
the eternal danger question. Once you have learned the soulwinning plan and have implemented it to win several to the Lord, it
becomes incredibly simple. Truthfully, the most consistent responses
you will hear will be in the category of, *I've tried to be a good person*
or *I've tried to live a good life.* The other examples I included are to
prepare you for the unexpected and to not be thrown off by these
kinds of responses from an unbeliever. When you completely know
your soulwinning plan, you will be prepared for anything.

Because of the strategy in the soulwinning plan, unsaved people
are comfortable and will reveal what they think. For that reason,
a believer's success will have a lot to do with how they handle the
responses to the eternal danger question in the plan. Just as they
will hear what you say to them, they will observe how you listen to
what they say to you They will always recognize that, as you follow
this plan, you are handling them in a diplomatic way.

As previously mentioned, you are an ambassador for Christ (2
Corinthians 5:20); therefore, always be diplomatic. Some unbelievers may say something just to see how you react. Do not react in
an emotional, negative way. Experienced and seasoned diplomats

do not react; they respond. Believers should respond with softness and clarity of direction. Do not confront and make a *big deal* out of their response. With the transitions tactic you can casually brush the responses aside and guide them into and through the gospel scriptures. It will be rare at this point, but if they try to ask questions, handle them in the same casual manner. Since you know the plan sequence, you can always come back to where you were when they interrupted you. Remember, you are in charge, so learn to stay in charge.

## I Can or I Can't—The Choice Is Yours

Winning souls is an exciting command and goal to follow. That is why doing the work of an evangelist is the way to fulfill all that Christ has for us in life. The release point of a fulfilled life of ministry includes winning souls. Many in the body of Christ spend years desperately searching for their own *ministry*. This is the opportunity you have been searching for in seeking God's will and ministry direction for your life, but it will never happen unless you try. We all must take a step of faith in winning souls to Christ.

The person who says, *I can learn to win souls and will do so* is correct. The person who says, *I can't learn to win souls and so I won't* is also correct. What we decide we can or cannot do is what we will do. The question here is which decision to make, which road to take, the road of *I can and will* or *I can't and won't*. The truth is you can; you just haven't done it yet.

### Make the winning decision

Now that you have read the *Witnessing Winzone*, you are going to have to make a decision. It will be a decision that says either, *I can do this!* or *I can't do this*. Both answers are correct based upon your choice. Let me argue for the *I can* answer for just a moment. Anyone can say *I can't* and if that is their decision, that is the end of the matter. More than likely, that decision will end any interest in learning to win souls. If you say, *I can*, that simple step of faith will take you into a life of personal fruitfulness in ministry beyond anything you felt was possible for yourself.

If you are willing to say *I can* you are going to have to spend a little time memorizing and committing to using your new plan. Memorize and know the sequence so well that your flow of conversation will make an unsaved person believe this is what you have known and understood all of your life. The reality is that the presentation is based upon biblical truth that you already know.

Armed with your new plan, you will understand witnessing in the context of uniquely handling unbelievers by uniquely handling the Word of God. The plan may appear to be a lot to learn and absorb, but in reality is quite brief.

## RIGHTEOUS BELIEVERS STILL NEED TRAINING

Believers are encouraged to live consecrated lives, witness, share their faith and win unsaved people to Christ. Some are taught that living a righteous and holy life is all that is necessary to win souls. The logic is that in doing so, unbelievers will then want to be like them. I think all believers will agree that no matter what a believer is involved in, they should live holy and righteous lives. What needs to be added to that understanding is specific instruction about how to win souls. All believers should understand that living a consecrated life in Christ is elementary for any successful life in Him. Millions of believers live holy and righteous lives but still have no clue about how to win an unsaved person to Jesus Christ. the *Witnessing Winzone* model has proved to be an extremely successful way to win souls while living a holy and consecrated life in Christ.

## YOU ARE A FULL-TIME MINISTER

Jesus Christ has a calling for every Christian, as declared by Jesus in John 15:16:

You did not choose Me, but I chose you and appointed you that you should go and bear fruit, and that your fruit should remain, that whatever you ask the Father in My name He may give you.

Every Christian should consider that he or she is in full time ministry. To say that only pastors and evangelists who are employed by and receive income through the church are fulltime ministers is inaccurate. If every blessing, including finances, is from God, then the income that any believer receives is from Him. The only difference is the place of service where He chooses to use believers. Some get their income through a church and others get their income from the job or business where God has placed them. It is the will of God that leads, guides, shapes and places believers in life's pursuits. It is a spiritual reality that all believers are fulltime, paid ministers in the co-shared ministry of fulfilling the Great Commission.

The true ministers are the believers who live out their lives throughout the highways and byways of the world as witnesses and ministers of Jesus Christ. Believers cannot neglect working for the Lord because they consider only pastors or church staff to be "full-time workers" for the Lord.

## SOULWINNING SUCCESS COMES QUICKLY

A young man recently attended one of my soulwinning seminars and said he had been searching for an effective way to witness to the unsaved. Over a six month period, he has led 21 people to Jesus Christ as Savior. He has used the *Witnessing Winzone* plan over and over again and says it never fails him. He is excited about becoming a soulwinner and realizing that the Lord is using him. The very first person he won to Christ was his own mother on the telephone.

## THE ROOT OF WITNESSING PROCRASTINATION CAN END

After you have led several people to Christ you will be so excited that you will barely be able to contain yourself. Take the short time it takes to get you started, and stop procrastinating in your responsibility for personal evangelism. Procrastination is simply putting things off to a later time. No one likes to be called a procrastinator. A root problem for procrastinators is often living in a state of aloneness, with no one else to encourage them or assist them in moving forward. The result is that nothing gets done, because there is no accountability and it is easy to postpone doing things. If that is your situation, I commit to being your partner in helping you get started in personal evangelism. I will pray every day for everyone who reads this book. With my partnership, support and prayers, I know that you can master this soulwinning plan and be successful.

Everyone needs people and everyone needs help. This strategic biblical soulwinning plan is the help you have been looking for; so take the step and give it a try. The Lord will meet you as you do and your life will be changed forever as you help change lives forever.

## PLAN YOUR WORK AND WORK YOUR PLAN

Pray and plan means pray and prepare! That is the surest way for you to become a successful soulwinner. If you will give two to three hours of committed, concentrated dedication to study, learn, memorize, and know through and through the *Witnessing Winzone* plan, you will become successful in winning souls. After you have led several to the Lord you will have an *Ah-Ha* type experience: *The light will come on...The day will dawn...YOU WILL GET IT!* All of a sudden things click, and you will see and completely understand what you are doing. After you have won several to Christ you will have become "closure-minded" and realize that you have indeed become a soulwinner.

Learn this soulwinning plan exactly as it has been presented in this book. Don't try to "outsmart it" by making adjustments until you have led at least twenty-five unsaved people to salvation using the plan. The more experienced you become, the more you will learn how to make some creative and appropriate adjustments. Adjustments always depend on the unsaved person and the situation you are in with that unsaved person. There is more than one way to win a person to Christ, once you know how. Make no mistake, this plan will absolutely give you that know-how.

## GIVE GOD SOMETHING HE CAN USE

Several years ago, I was a member of First Baptist Houston in Houston, Texas, pastored by Dr. John Bisagno, a great pastor and preacher with a heart for souls. I realized one Sunday morning that I was going to be late to church; there was no way I could get to church on time, since I lived about twenty to twenty-five minutes away. On this particular Sunday I decided to look in the yellow pages and I found Easthaven Baptist Church, which was only minutes from my apartment. I visited the church that morning, filled out the visitor card, and the next day received a call from Pastor Buford Cain, the pastor of the church. He offered to come to my apartment to visit me, but I responded that I would come to the church to see him, and did so.

As we visited, he asked about what I was doing at First Baptist Houston. I had to admit that for the most part I was just attending, "warming a seat." At that time I had been saved about two years. Pastor Cain asked me what I thought I should be doing and I couldn't answer him. He then gave me some of the best advice I have ever received in my life. Pastor Cain said to me, "Brent, you have to give God something He can use."

The Lord used the impact of that advice to immediately launch me on a journey that ultimately led me to become a pastor and author this book. Pastor Cain was correct; believers must give God something He can use, even when we don't really know what it is and don't feel like it. It is easy to think, *Let others do it!* or *It's too much for me!* or *I'm not really lazy; I just don't want to get involved!* or *I don't want to be rejected!* or *I'm afraid of what someone might say to me!* or *This is not my gift!* or *It's not that I am over emotional, I just don't feel like it.* or *I just don't know what to say!* Excuses will never stop unless we stop using them.

The bottom line is that in personal evangelism everyone has to start somewhere, and this soulwinning plan is an incredible way to get started. I encourage you to take Pastor Cain's advice, as I did. Get equipped, go for it and give God something He can use! The apostle Paul declared in Philippians 3:13–14:

> Brethren, I do not count myself to have apprehended; but one thing I do, forgetting those things which are behind and reaching forward to those things which are ahead, I press toward the goal for the prize of the upward call of God in Christ Jesus.

## MAY GOD BLESS YOU

With all my heart I hope and pray that you are a great success in fulfilling your God-given ministry to win souls. When you learn and follow this soulwinning plan, you will become one of the most consistent soulwinners in the history of the body of Christ. I know that sounds like a bold statement, but it will be true. I further know that Jesus is in this unique soulwinning plan because it is focused on presenting His salvation gospel. He will be in it with you and you will absolutely become successful in personal evangelism. Whoever you are and no matter where you are, I will pray every day for your life and your success in personal evangelism. My heart is to see millions equipped to win millions more to Christ. I know that someday we will all meet in heaven and I so much want to meet you and the many souls you won to Jesus Christ.

We only go through this short life one time and I want your time and mine to count for something great in the kingdom of God. Opportunities to be a part of something significant in the body of Christ do not come often and learning how to win souls

167

is very significant. There is an exciting opportunity before you now and I hope you take full advantage of it. My prayer for you is that you fulfill God's plan and purpose for your life, and that you become the man or woman that our heavenly Father wants you to be. I pray that there will be countless opportunities for you to simply say to some unsaved person, *You know, I talk to a lot of people about Jesus Christ, salvation, and eternal life. Do you mind if I ask you a question without being too personal?*

# Notes

## Chapter 3
## The Witnessing Winzone Analysis

1. The subject of Jesus being raised from the dead as introduced in Romans 10:9 is not discussed except as it is referred to when explaining Rom 6:23. Because it is not deeply dealt with here, do not take that to mean that I do not believe in His bodily resurrection. I absolutely do, because if there is no resurrection, there is no Savior. The main reason it is not discussed at this point is because most people are generally familiar with the story of His resurrection, and it is not necessary to offer an in-depth explanation in order to win the unsaved person to Christ. A witnessing conversation about His resurrection would open up a much longer and unnecessary conversation. A more complete explanation of the death, burial and resurrection of Jesus Christ is always dealt with in a discipling context.

## Chapter 9
## Relational, Flexible, and Equipped

1. *Webster's Ninth New Collegiate Dictionary* (Springfield, Massachusetts: Merriam-Webster Inc., Publishers, 1990), 1104
2. Ibid., 1355

# To Contact the Author

drbrentprice@verizon.net